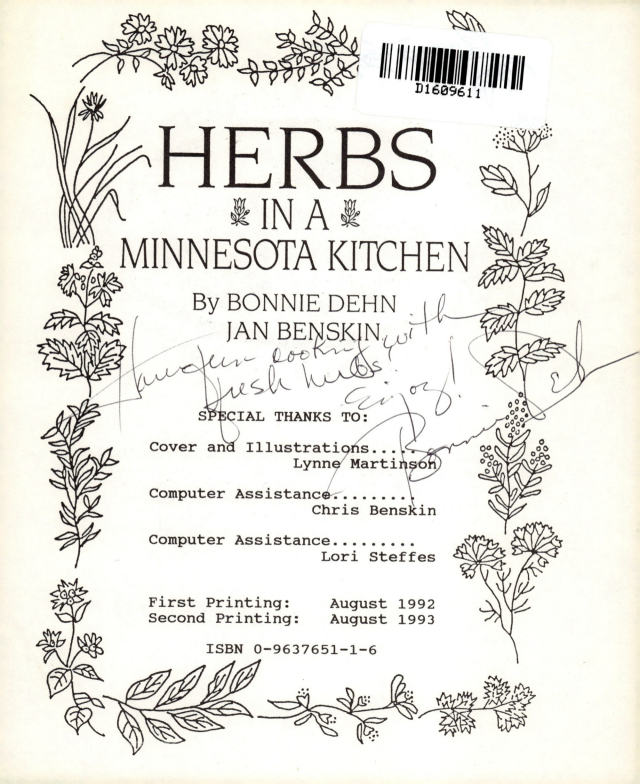

# HERBS
## IN A
## MINNESOTA KITCHEN

### By BONNIE DEHN
### JAN BENSKIN

SPECIAL THANKS TO:

Cover and Illustrations.....
Lynne Martinson

Computer Assistance........
Chris Benskin

Computer Assistance........
Lori Steffes

First Printing:      August 1992
Second Printing:     August 1993

ISBN 0-9637651-1-6

# Dehn's Garden

## Fresh Herbs & Vegetables

Dehn's Garden is a family farm of approximately 100 acres of specialty crops and greenhouses. 35 acres are devoted to producing herbs. Dehn's Garden supplies herbs to local grocery stores and restaurants. They also sell fresh herbs, vegetables, plants, and flowers at the Minneapolis Farmer's Market.

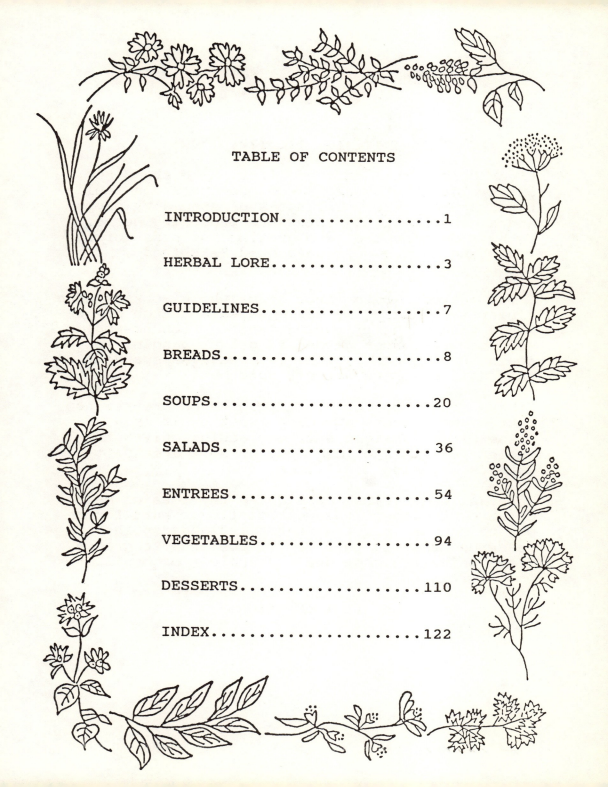

# TABLE OF CONTENTS

# A NOTE FROM BONNIE

Fresh herbs are a part of life.  My husband Bob, our two daughters, and I own and operate a family farm, approximately 100 acres of specialty crops and greenhouses.  35 acres are producing herbs. We have been in the herb growing business for 15 years and have always advocated SAFE food production.

I was introduced to fresh herbs while working at a flower shop during my college years.  Each day we would take turns preparing lunch.  Frances would send me out to her garden to get a "handful" of one herb or another.  The interest was sparked; to this day, the fire has not gone out.

I have found cooking with fresh herbs creates new tastes and flavors any dish, whether it is a casserole or a light entrée.  Adding chives to omelets or mint to iced teas or soft drinks creates exciting new tastes.

When Jan and I first considered the idea of a cookbook together, the most difficult part for me was to convert all the "handfuls" and "sprigs" to measurements.  To this day, I continue to grab a "few" chives to chop and a "handful" of basil.

My advice to using fresh herbs?--There are no limits, only wonderful creations!

# A NOTE FROM JAN

I'm rather new to the world of herbs.  Although
I've used herbs in teas for many years, I only
began growing herbs a few years ago, starting with
containers of parsley and chives on the porch.  As
I discovered the flavor that fresh herbs add to
food, my herbs overflowed from the porch into the
garden.  I'm amazed at the variety of herbs
available; some were unknown to me until I met
Bonnie.  I'm intrigued with the edible flowers and
keep experimenting with new ways to use them.  My
husband Bryan and son Chris have been pleased with
all the "weeds" I've added to our cuisine.

I began cooking when I was eight years old from a
<u>Kid's Cookbook</u> given to me by my father.  I
learned cooking skills from my mother and
grandmother, both excellent cooks.  My interest
has continued and developed into a strong
avocation.  I enjoy anything related to food-
cooking, entertaining, and attending cooking
classes.  I also collect cookbooks and still have
the one I received as an 8-year-old.  I've written
two cookbooks <u>Teatime Treats</u> and <u>More Teatime
Treats</u> as donations to the annual Share Fair at
Faith Lutheran Church in Coon Rapids.

When Bonnie and I met, we thought it would be fun
to pool our recipes and share them with others.
We offer this cookbook in the hope that you, too,
will enjoy cooking with fresh herbs.  From our
kitchens to yours, we wish you Happy Herbal
Cooking!

# HERB CHART

ARUGALA..........spicy, nutty flavor that adds
                 spark to salads and stir fry
BASIL............fresh, sweet, subtle flavor, use
                 in tomato and pasta dishes,
                 pesto, vegetables, and soups
CHERVIL..........add to fish sauces, potato
                 salads, and scrambled eggs
CHIVES...........mild onion flavor, use as
                 accents for salads, stir
                 fry, omelets, and egg dishes
CILANTRO.........a must for salsas, curry, stir
                 fry, Oriental and Mexican
                 dishes
DILL.............light dilly flavor, use in fish
                 sauces, vegetable dips,
                 serve with fresh potatoes
                 and vegetables
GARLIC CHIVES.....great garlic flavor to comple-
                 ment garlic toast, sautéed
                 vegetables and marinades
ITALIAN PARSLEY...flavors soups, stews, pasta
                 sauces, etc.
LEMON GRASS.......creates a lemon flavor for stir
                 fry and soups, also makes
                 great tea
LEMON THYME.......adds a light lemon flavor to
                 chicken and fish when
                 grilled

CONTINUED ON NEXT PAGE.....

# HERB CHART

MARJORAM.........a delightful addition to poultry
                   stuffings, egg dishes and
                   vegetables
MINT.............sweet spearmint flavor, use in
                   cool summer drinks, sweet
                   peas, and new potatoes
OREGANO..........a must for pasta, spaghetti
                   sauces, pizza, favorite
                   Italian dishes
ROSEMARY.........flavors chicken, marinades, baked
                   meats and fish
SAGE.............complements poultry, dressings,
                   sausages, lamb, and veal
SAVORY...........adds an unusual sweet flavor to
                   green vegetables
SORREL...........a tart taste to compliment cream
                   sauces and fish; adds fun to
                   salads
TARRAGON.........light anise flavor, add to wine,
                   vinegars, chicken, and beef
                   stroganoff
THYME............complements vegetables, soups,
                   breads, and meats
WATERCRESS.......light snappy flavor, accents
                   salads and sandwiches

# HERBAL TEAS

Herbal teas were first used as medicine, but are now consumed as beverages by choice. Herbal teas can be a tasty alternative when attempting to limit caffeine.

Mint teas are delicious and many flavors of mint are available - chocolate, orange, lime, spearmint, applemint and peppermint. Chamomile (flower heads instead of leaves), sage, lemon verbena, lemon grass, lemon balm, raspberry leaves, and rosemary also make delicious teas. (Check a reputable herbal before experimenting. Some herbs are not suitable for tea and could make you ill.)

Prepare herbal tea by pouring boiling water over a handful of herbal leaves (washed well) in a pottery teapot. Allow to steep 5 minutes before serving. Extend your herbal usage by brewing a pot of tea to accompany the delicious bread and desserts in this book!

# FLOWERS IN THE KITCHEN

No longer are flowers only part of our kitchen decor. We admire their appearance as well as their flavor as we use them in cooking and baking. Flowers are a beautiful garnish but can also be used in other ways:

1) Mince and add to cream cheese and butter.

2) Whole blossoms can be tossed in a salad or sprinkled on top of a composed salad.

3) Add to fruit salad and garnish with mint.

4) Float in drinks or cold soups.

5) Mince and use in baking.

Use only tender young blossoms that have been rinsed and patted dry. Use flowers from your own garden or commercial flowers marketed as edible flowers (nontoxic and chemical-free). These can be found in the produce department of your grocery store. The following is a partial list of edible flowers. (Check with a reputable source before using others.)

Chive blossom
Lilac
Nasturtium
Rose
Violet
Daylily
Fuchsia
Hollyhock

Lavendar
Marigold
Pansy
Squash blossom
Dandelion
Forget-me-not
Geranium
Impatiens

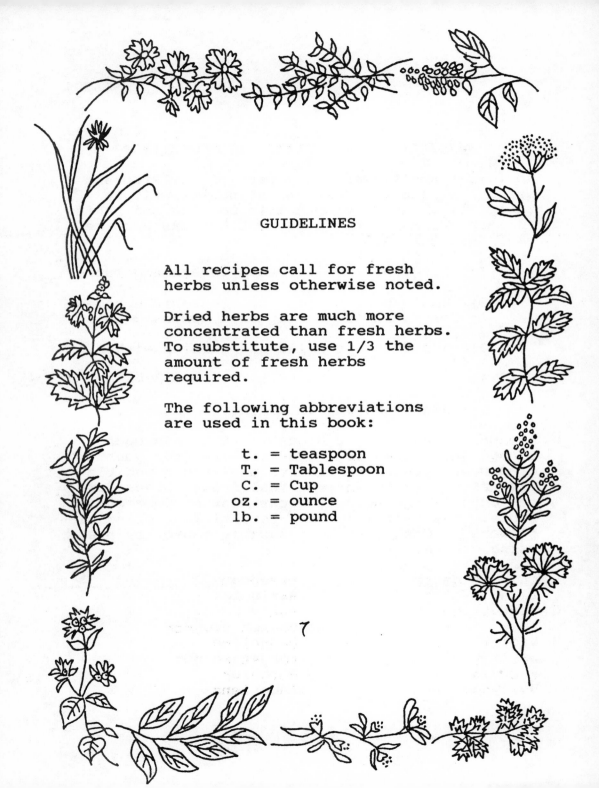

# GUIDELINES

All recipes call for fresh
herbs unless otherwise noted.

Dried herbs are much more
concentrated than fresh herbs.
To substitute, use 1/3 the
amount of fresh herbs
required.

The following abbreviations
are used in this book:

      t. = teaspoon
      T. = Tablespoon
      C. = Cup
    oz. = ounce
    lb. = pound

BREADS

# DROP CHIVE BISCUITS

|         |      |                |
|--------:|------|----------------|
| 2       | C.   | flour          |
| 1       | t.   | salt           |
| 2       | t.   | baking powder  |
| 1/2     | t.   | soda           |
| 6       | T.   | butter         |
| 1 1/2   | C.   | buttermilk     |
| 3       | T.   | chopped chives |

Sift dry ingredients (except chives) into a bowl.
Using a pastry blender, cut in butter.  Add chives
and milk, stirring with fork until combined.  Drop
by large tablespoonfuls onto a greased pan.  Bake
at 450 degress for 12-15 minutes or until lightly
browned.

Have fresh chives all year long — keep a chive plant by your kitchen window.

# SAGE CORNMEAL BISCUITS

```
1 1/2 C.    flour
  1/2 C.    cornmeal
  1/2 t.    salt
    4 t.    baking powder
  1/2 t.    cream of tartar
  1/2 C.    butter
  2/3 C.    milk
    2 T.    chopped sage
```

Sift dry ingredients (except sage) into a bowl.
Using a pastry blender, cut in butter. Add sage
and milk. Stir with fork until dough combines.
Knead on floured board. Roll 1/2-inch thick and
cut with floured cutter. Place on ungreased
cookie sheet. Bake in preheated 425 degree oven
for 15 minutes or until browned.

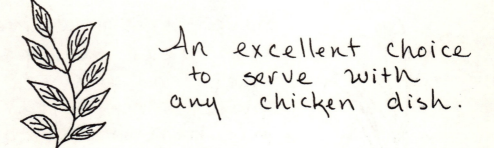

An excellent choice
to serve with
any chicken dish.

# ROSEMARY RAISIN MUFFINS

| | | |
|---|---|---|
| 1/2 | C. | butter, softened |
| 3/4 | C. | sugar |
| 2 | | eggs |
| 2 | C. | flour |
| 1 | t. | baking soda |
| 1/2 | t. | salt |
| 1 | C. | buttermilk |
| 1 | C. | golden raisins |
| 1 | T. | grated orange peel |
| 2 | T. | fresh minced rosemary |
| 1/4 | t. | cinnamon |
| 1/4 | C. | orange juice |

Cream butter and sugar. Beat in eggs. Sift together flour, soda, and salt. Add to butter mixture alternately with buttermilk. Stir in raisins, orange peel, and rosemary. Spoon the batter into greased miniature muffin pans. Bake in preheated 375 degree oven for 10-13 minutes until light brown. Remove from oven and brush tops of muffins with orange juice. Turn out onto rack and cool completely.

Marvelous with a cup of spiced tea !

# DILL CHEESE BREAD

| | | |
|---|---|---|
| 2 | C. | flour |
| 2 | t. | baking powder |
| 1 | T. | sugar |
| 3/4 | t. | salt |
| 1/4 | C. | butter |
| 1 | C. | grated Cheddar cheese |
| 1 | T. | minced onion |
| 1 | T. | dill seed |
| 3/4 | C. | milk |
| 1 | | egg |

Combine flour, baking powder, sugar, and salt in
bowl.  Add butter and blend with pastry blender.
Stir in cheese, onion, and dill.  Whisk milk and
egg in another bowl.  Add to other ingredients and
stir just until moistened.  Pour into greased 8
1/2 x 4 1/2-inch bread pan. Bake in preheated 350
degree oven for 40-45 minutes or until browned.
Cool 10 minutes in pan.  Invert onto rack and cool
completely.

*Perfect with tomato soup.*

# GARLIC BREAD

| | |
|---|---|
| 1 | loaf french bread |
| 1/2 C. | softened butter |
| 1 T. | chopped Italian parsley |
| 3 T. | chopped garlic chives |

Blend together butter and herbs. Slice French
bread lengthwise. Lay flat and spread butter
mixture on each half. Broil at 400 degrees for
10-12 minutes.

Serve with any
Italian favorites —
Lasagna, Spaghetti,
etc.

# HERBED CHEESE BREAD

| | |
|---|---|
| 2-3 | loaves of French bread |
| 2 T. | chopped garlic chives |
| 4 T. | chopped chives |
| 2 T. | chopped Italian parsley |
| 4 T. | olive oil |
| 1 C. | butter, softened |
| 1 C. | grated Parmesan cheese |
| 1 t. | freshly ground pepper |
| | dash of salt |

Have ingredients at room temperature. Combine all
ingredients and mix well. Chill for several
hours. Slice bread and spread mixture on each
slice. Reassemble the loaves and wrap each loaf
in foil. Bake in preheated 375 oven until heated
through.

Perfect with
Spaghetti !

# DILLY ROLLS

| 1 | loaf frozen bread dough |
|---|---|
| 4 T. | butter (or cream cheese) |
| 3 T. | chopped fresh dill |
| 1/2 T. | Italian parsley |

Thaw dough; roll into an oblong measuring 8x5 inches. Spread butter across surface; sprinkle with dill and Italian parsley. Roll lengthwise and slice in 2" rolls. Place into greased 8x8-inch pan. Bake in preheated 350 degree oven for 30 minutes.

Lavender's blue, dilly, dilly, lavender's green,
When I am King, dilly, dilly, you shall be Queen.
Who told you so, dilly, dilly, who told you so?
'Twas my own heart, dilly, dilly, that told me so.

— Traditional

# HERBED PASTA

| | |
|---|---|
| 2/3 C. | flour |
| | dash of salt |
| 1 | egg, beaten |
| 1 t. | finely chopped oregano |
| | (can substitute thyme or |
| | Italian parsley) |

Combine ingredients and knead together.  Cover
bowl for 1/2 hour. Roll out very, very thin.  Cut
and dry.


# HERBED EGG NOODLES

| | |
|---|---|
| 2 | eggs |
| 1/4 t. | salt |
| 1 1/2 C. | flour |
| 1 T. | finely chopped dill (or 2 T. basil) |

Mix ingredients together.  Adjust flour, if
necessary, to make a workable dough.  Roll out to
dry a few minutes, then cut.  The herbs give pasta
a brand new flavor.


To sweeten pasta and rice, add
a sprig of rosemary to the cooking
water.

# FOCACCIA

| | |
|---|---|
| 1 | package dry yeast |
| 1 C. | warm water (105-115 degrees) |
| 3 T. | rosemary |
| 3 T. | olive oil |
| 2 t. | salt |
| 3 C. | flour |
| | olive oil |
| | freshly grated Parmesan cheese |

Dissolve yeast in warm water in large bowl. Stir in rosemary, oil, salt, and 2 1/2 C. flour. Knead dough on lightly floured surface, adding flour as needed. When smooth and elastic, place in greased bowl. Brush with oil and cover. Let rise until double (about 1 hour). Punch down and press in oiled 12-inch pizza pan. Brush with olive oil and sprinkle with cheese. Let rise another 30 minutes. Bake in preheated 400 degree for 20-25 minutes.

Serve with any Italian meal.

# HERB BREAD

| | | |
|---|---|---|
| 3 | C. | warm water (105-115 degrees) |
| 2 | | packages dry yeast |
| 1 | T. | salt |
| 1 | C. | powdered milk |
| 1/2 | C. | oil |
| 1/2 | C. | honey |
| 1 | C. | whole wheat flour |
| 1 | C. | 7-grain flour |
| 1 | C. | cornmeal |
| 5 | C. | bread flour |
| 1/2 | C. | chopped fresh herbs |
| | | (combination: sage, basil, dill) |

Pour 2 1/2 C. water into a large bowl. To the
remaining 1/2 C. water, add 2 packages dry yeast;
stir to dissolve. Set aside. To the water in the
large bowl, add powdered milk and salt. Stir.
Add oil and honey. Stir in dissolved yeast. Add
whole wheat flour, 7-grain flour, and cornmeal.
Stir in herbs. Add bread flour, stirring in 1 C.
at a time. Let dough rest 10 minutes. Turn out
on floured board and knead until smooth, adding
more flour as needed. Put in buttered bowl,
butter top, and cover with plastic wrap. Let rise
until doubled, about 1 1/2 hours. Punch down and
divide into 4 equal parts. Shape into free-form
loaves and put on greased cookie sheets. Butter
tops and cover with plastic wrap. Let rise until
doubled. Bake in preheated 375 degree oven for
35-40 minutes. Turn out on cooling rack and brush
with melted butter.

# HERBED BUTTERS:

## PARSLEY AND THYME BUTTER

```
    1 t.    chopped Italian parsley,
    1 t.    chopped thyme
  1/2 C.    soft butter (1 stick)
```

## CHIVE BUTTER

```
    1 T.    chopped chives
  1/2 C.    soft butter
```

## LEMON BASIL

```
    1 T.    chopped lemon basil
  1/2 C.    soft butter
```

## DILL

```
    1 T.    chopped dill
  1/2 C.    soft butter
(excellent with green beans)
```

## HERB BUTTER

| | |
|---|---|
| 2 C. | softened butter |
| 2 T. | parsley |
| 2 T. | thyme |
| 2 T. | chives |
| 1 T. | dill |
| 1 T. | marjoram |
| 1 T. | chervil |
| 1 t. | lemon juice |

Chop and bruise all herbs.  Combine lemon juice, herbs, and butter.  Mix well and refrigerate. This butter may also be frozen.


## CREAM CHEESE WITH CHIVES AND LEMON BASIL

| | |
|---|---|
| 1 | (8 oz.) package cream cheese |
| 3 T. | chopped chives |
| 4 T. | chopped lemon basil |

Soften cream cheese.  Blend the chives and lemon basil.  Serve with bagel sticks or crackers.

19

SOUPS

# HEARTY BEAN SOUP

|          |       |                          |
|----------|-------|--------------------------|
| 1 lb.    |       | dry navy beans           |
| 8 C.     |       | water                    |
| 1 C.     |       | chopped onion            |
| 1 C.     |       | chopped celery           |
| 1 C.     |       | sliced carrots           |
| 1/4 C.   |       | chopped parsley          |
| 1 1/2 t. |       | salt                     |
| 1/2 t.   |       | pepper                   |
| 1 T.     |       | chopped basil            |
| 1 T.     |       | chopped oregano          |
| 1 lb.    |       | ham hocks or 1 ham bone  |

Soak beans overnight; drain. Combine all
ingredients in crockpot. Cook 10-12 hours at low
setting or 5-6 hours at high setting. Remove ham
bone or ham hocks. Trim off meat and add to soup.

Team with a
loaf of brown bread—
a delicious meal on
a blustery day!

# BEER CHEESE SOUP

|        |                        |
|--------|------------------------|
| 4 T.   | butter                 |
| 1/4 C. | chopped celery         |
| 1/2 C  | chopped onions         |
| 1/4 C. | carrots, chopped fine  |
| 5 T.   | flour                  |
| 1/2 t. | paprika                |
| 1/2 t. | dry mustard.           |
| 1/2 C. | beer                   |
| 1 C.   | chicken broth          |
| 1 C.   | grated American cheese |
| 1 C.   | grated Cheddar cheese  |
| 2 T.   | chopped dill           |
| 2 T.   | chopped parsley        |
| 1 C.   | "half & half"          |
| 1/4 t. | tabasco sauce          |

Sauté carrots, onions, and celery in butter until
tender.  Stir in flour.  Cook on low heat 3-4
minutes. (Don't brown).  Stir in paprika, dry
mustard, beer, and chicken broth.  With wire
whisk, whip until smooth.  Add cheese and dill.
Bring to a boil and let simmer 5-10 minutes.
Remove from heat and stir in "half & half",
parsley, and tabasco sauce.

Dill and cheese
a great combination.

# CREAMY CARROT SOUP

|          |      |                             |
|----------|------|-----------------------------|
| 1-1/2    | C.   | onions, chopped             |
| 4        |      | carrots, sliced             |
| 1        |      | clove garlic, minced        |
| 1/2      | t.   | ground black pepper         |
| 1        | T.   | chopped cinnamon basil      |
| 1        | T.   | chopped Italian parsley     |
| 2        | T.   | butter                      |
| 6        | C.   | chicken broth               |
| 3/4      | C.   | quick rice                  |
| 3/4      | C.   | whole milk                  |
|          |      | shredded carrot (optional)  |

In a stock pot, sauté carrots, garlic, pepper, and
Italian parsley in butter for 1 minute over medium
heat.  Add broth and rice.  Bring to a boil.
Cover, reduce heat and simmer for 30 minutes until
the carrots and rice are tender.  Remove from
heat.  Carefully fill a blender container with
half of the cooked vegetable and rice mixture and
blend into a smooth purée.  Pour purée into
another pot and repeat purée procedure with
remaining vegetable and rice mixture. When all the
mixture has been puréed, stir in the milk and heat
to a simmer.  If desired, garnish with a small
amount of shredded carrot.

# EASY CHILI

| 1 1/2 lb. | ground beef |
|---|---|
| 1/2 C. | chopped onion |
| 1 t. | salt |
| 1 T. | chili powder |
| 2 | (15 1/2 oz.) cans kidney beans |
| 1 | (15 oz.) can tomato sauce |
| 1/4 C. | chopped cilantro |
| 2 T. | chopped oregano |
| 1/2 t. | cumin |

Brown ground beef and onion; drain.  Add remaining
ingredients.  Bring to a boil.  Reduce heat and
simmer 45 minutes, stirring occasionally.

Serve in pottery
soup bowls and
garnish with cheddar
cheese and sprigs
of cilantro.

# THE BEST DARN OL' CHILI

|        |                                                  |
| ------ | ------------------------------------------------ |
| 1 lb.  | ground beef                                      |
| 1      | chopped onion                                    |
| 3 T.   | chopped garlic chives                            |
| 2      | (28 oz.) cans stewed tomatoes                    |
| 1/2 C. | chopped celery                                   |
| 1      | chopped green pepper                             |
| 4      | sliced Anaheim chili peppers (mildly hot)        |
| 3      | (15 1/2 oz.) cans kidney beans (Caliente beans for more heat) |

Brown the ground beef, onion, and chives. Combine with remaining ingredients in a large kettle (at least 6 quarts). Simmer for at least 45 minutes. Serve with corn bread and honey.

Want more heat in your chili? Adding 2-3 chopped jalapeño peppers will knock your socks off!

# GAZPACHO

|        |      |                                                    |
|--------|------|----------------------------------------------------|
| 2      |      | ripe tomatoes                                      |
| 1      |      | cucumber (peeled if skin is bitter or waxed)       |
| 1      |      | green pepper                                       |
| 1      |      | clove garlic, minced                               |
| 3/4    | C.   | mixed herbs: (Italian parsley, basil, thyme, chives) |
| 1      | T.   | olive oil                                          |
| 3      | T.   | lemon juice                                        |
| 2      | C.   | chilled water or vegetable stock                   |
| 1      |      | onion, sliced thinly                               |
|        |      | dry bread crumbs or yogurt                         |

Chop the vegetables very fine.  Slowly add oil, lemon juice, and water or stock.  Add onion. Chill 4 hours before serving.  Garnish with dry bread crumbs or yogurt.


Serve gazpacho for the first course when serving tacos for dinner.  Or, for a special luncheon, scoop out large, firm red tomatoes, fill them with gazpacho, and top with sour cream or yogurt seasoned with curry.  Set each tomato on a big Romaine leaf and pass the croutons.

# LEMON RICE SOUP

|       |                                |
|-------|--------------------------------|
| 6 C.  | vegetable broth                |
| 1/2 C.| brown rice                     |
| 1     | bay leaf                       |
| 1 T.  | chopped Italian parsley        |
| 1 T.  | summer savory                  |
| 4     | eggs, beaten                   |
|       | juice and grated peel of 2 lemons |
|       | minced green onions or chives  |

Heat stock to boiling; add rice, bay leaf, and
salt if needed. Simmer 30-40 minutes or until
rice is tender. Remove bay leaf. Mix summer
savory with beaten eggs. Add lemon juice and
grated peel and mix again. Slowly add one cup of
stock to egg mixture, stirring constantly. Add
egg mixture to soup. Garnish each bowl with
minced green onions or chives before serving.

Serve lemon rice soup in
demitasse cups in the living
room before dinner. A
delicate appetite teaser!

# MUSHROOM AND POTATO SOUP

```
    6 T.     butter
1 1/2 lbs.  fresh oyster mushrooms
    1 C.     minced onion
1 1/2 lbs.  potatoes (about 6 small
                boiling potatoes)
    6 C.     basic stock
    1 t.     salt
  1/4 C.     finely chopped celery
  1/4 C.     finely chopped green onion,
                including tops
    2 T.     chopped fresh parsley
    1 T.     chopped fresh dill
    1 C.     sour cream
            freshly ground pepper
```

Wipe mushrooms with damp towel and slice
lengthwise 1/8-inch thick.  Melt 4 T. butter in a
heavy 5-quart enameled or stainless kettle.  When
foam subsides, add mushrooms and onions, stirring
well.  Partially cover and simmer 20 minutes.
Meanwhile peel potatoes and slice 1/4-inch thick.
Add stock, potatoes, and salt, and bring to a
boil.  Reduce heat and cook partially covered
until potatoes are tender but intact (about 45
minutes).  In a large heavy skillet, melt 2 T.
butter; add onions, celery, and parsley.  Cook
uncovered, stirring frequently over low heat until
celery is tender but not brown (about 15 minutes).
Combine 1/2 C. boiling soup stock with sour cream
and mix well.  Slowly pour this into the skillet,
stirring constantly; raise heat and bring to a
boil.  Add this to the soup and stir throughly.
Correct seasonings, and serve sprinkled with dill
and freshly ground pepper.  Serves 6-8

# POTATO BACON SOUP

|  |  |  |
|---|---|---|
| 3 | C. | diced potatoes |
| 2 | C. | chicken broth |
| 1/2 | C. | diced celery |
| 5 |  | slices bacon, browned and chopped |
| 1/2 | T. | chervil |
| 1/2 | T. | Italian parsley |
| 2 | C. | milk |
| 2 | T. | butter |

Simmer potatoes in chicken broth until nearly
done.  Add the remaining ingredients; simmer until
the potatoes are cooked.  Add milk and butter.  To
thicken the soup, stir in small amounts of dried
potato flakes.

Chervil ⌐
    a great favorite
in french kitchens.

# FRESH TOMATO SOUP

```
    2 lbs.  tomatoes
  1/4 C.    chopped onion
  1/4 C.    chopped green pepper
  1/4 C.    chopped celery
    2 T.    chopped Italian parsley
    2 T.    chopped basil
    1 T.    sugar
            salt and pepper
```

Remove stem end and peel tomatoes.  Cut into small
wedges.  Combine all ingredients in a saucepan
over medium heat.  Cover and bring to a boil.
Simmer 10 minutes.

# TOMATO SOUP WITH FRESH BASIL

|        |                                                      |
|--------|------------------------------------------------------|
| 3 T.   | butter                                               |
| 1      | large onion, sliced                                  |
| 1      | large carrot, shredded                               |
| 4      | large tomatoes, peeled, seeded, and coarsely chopped (about 4 C.) |
| 1/4 C. | packed, chopped basil leaves                         |
| 2 T.   | chopped Italian parsley                              |
| 1/2 t. | salt                                                 |
| 3/4 t. | sugar                                                |
| 1/8 t. | white pepper                                         |
| 1      | (14 oz.) can regular-strength chicken broth          |
| 1 C.   | pasta                                                |

In a 3 to 4-quart pan over medium heat, melt
butter. Add onion and carrot; cook until onion is
limp. Stir in tomatoes, basil, parsley, salt,
sugar, and pepper. Bring to a boil over high
heat, stirring. Cover, reduce heat, and simmer
for 10 minutes. Purée mixture and set aside. In
a small pan over high heat, bring broth to a boil.
Add pasta, reduce heat to medium, and cook until
tender (about 7 minutes). Stir tomato purée into
broth and heat to simmering. Makes about 6 cups.

# VEGETABLE BEEF STEW

| | | |
|---|---|---|
| 1 1/2 lbs. | stew meat |
| 1 C. | sliced carrots |
| 1 C. | chopped celery |
| 1 C. | chopped onions |
| | salt and pepper |
| 2 | beef bouillon cubes |
| 1/4 C. | barley |
| 1 1/2 C. | water |
| 2 | (6 oz.) cans V-8 juice |
| 1/4 C. | chopped parsley |
| 1/4 C. | chopped basil |
| 1 C. | frozen peas |

Combine all ingredients (except frozen peas) in a crock pot. Cook on high for 1 hour. Reduce to low and simmer all day. Add frozen peas 15 minutes before serving.

For those who dislike whole tomatoes in their soup.

# SIMPLE VEGETABLE STEW

|          |                                    |
|----------|------------------------------------|
| 1 C.     | carrots, peeled and cut in chunks  |
| 1        | medium onion, chopped              |
| 3 C.     | red potatoes, diced in large pieces |
| 1 C.     | chopped celery                     |
| 1/2 C.   | barley                             |
| 1 C.     | peas                               |
| 1 C.     | green beans                        |
| 1        | (28 oz.) can stewed tomatoes       |
| 3 T.     | chopped Italian parsley            |
| 1 T.     | basil                              |
| 1 T.     | chopped thyme                      |

Combine all ingredients in a soup pot (or a large crock pot).  Simmer, adding more liquid as needed. Before serving, use a corn starch paste or add small amounts of dried potato flakes to thicken if desired.

Chopped chives and watercress sprigs added to a sandwich will add freshness to any brown bag lunch!

# VEGETABLE SOUP WITH BASIL

|         |                                      |
|---------|--------------------------------------|
| 1       | quart regular-strength chicken broth |
| 1       | large tomato, peeled and coarsely chopped |
| 2 C.    | green beans, cut into 1-inch lengths |
| 2 C.    | potatoes, cut into 1/2-inch cubes    |
| 1/8 t.  | lemon pepper                         |
| 2 C.    | rotini                               |
|         | dash of salt                         |
| 1/4 C.  | chopped basil leaves                 |
| 2 T.    | garlic chives                        |
| 3 T.    | Italian parsley                      |
| 1 t.    | oregano                              |
| 1/4 C.  | salad oil                            |
| 3/4 C.  | shredded Swiss cheese                |

In a 4-quart pan over high heat, bring broth to a
boil.  Add tomato and juice, green beans,
potatoes, and pepper.  Cover, reduce heat, and
simmer for an hour.  Add rotini and cook until
tender (about 15 minutes).  Meanwhile, mix
together basil, chives, parsley, oregano, and
salad oil; place in a 3-quart warmed tureen.  Pour
in hot soup; gradually stir in cheese, adding 2 T.
at a time and mixing well after each addition.
Serve immediately.  Makes about 12 cups.

# PUMPKIN BOWL STEW

| | | |
|---|---|---|
| 1 | | medium pie pumpkin (pie pumpkins have thick, meaty sides) |
| 1 | C. | sliced carrots |
| 1 | C. | sliced parsnips |
| 1 | C. | chopped onion |
| 1 | C. | chopped celery |
| 1 | | (10 1/2 oz.) can chicken broth |
| 1/4 | t. | allspice |
| 2 | T. | chopped cinnamon basil |
| 1 | C. | diced potatoes |
| 3 | T. | Italian parsley |
| 1 | T. | chopped thyme |

Clean the pumpkin, remove the seeds, and scrape the inside. Reserve the "hat." Put the ingredients (uncooked) into the pumpkin. Place the pumpkin on a cookie sheet. Bake in a preheated 300 degree oven for 3-4 hours. The pumpkin and root vegetables will combine to make their own thickening.

Served in its own shell, pumpkin stew is a festive main course for Hallowe'en or Thanksgiving.

# WATERCRESS SOUP

|       |                             |
|-------|-----------------------------|
| 2 C.  | watercress (leaves and stems) |
| 2 C.  | chicken broth               |
| 1 T.  | Italian parsley             |
| 1 C.  | carrots, julienned          |
| 1 C.  | milk, scalded               |
| 1/2 C.| instant potato flakes       |

Steam watercress, chicken broth, carrots, and together until tender.  Add milk.  Heat but don't boil.  Add potato flakes to thicken.

 Serve hot on a cold, blustery day or cold as a summertime refresher.

SALADS

# BROCCOLI SALAD

|        |      |                             |
|--------|------|-----------------------------|
| 1      | lb.  | fresh broccoli florets      |
| 1      | C.   | shredded Cheddar cheese     |
| 1      | C.   | bacon, cooked and crumbled  |
| 1/4    | C.   | chopped dill                |
| 1/4    | C.   | chopped onion               |
| 1 1/2  | C.   | Hellman's mayonnaise        |
| 1      | T.   | sugar                       |
| 1/4    | C.   | white wine vinegar          |

Combine broccoli, cheese, bacon, dill, and onion.
Toss together and set aside. Combine other
ingredients. Blend into broccoli mix.

For a sweeter
salad ⌣ add raisins.

# SUNBURST CARROT SALAD

|       |      |                         |
|-------|------|-------------------------|
| 2     | C.   | grated carrots          |
| 1     | C.   | pineapple chunks        |
| 1     | C.   | mandarin orange sections |
| 1/2   | C.   | raisins                 |
| 2     | T.   | chopped mint            |
| 1/2   | C.   | grated coconut          |
| 1/2   | C.   | walnut pieces           |
| 4     | T.   | yogurt                  |

Mix all ingredients together. Serve on lettuce
leaves. This salad is best when it has been
refrigerated an hour or two before serving.

Mint adds color
as well as a "cool"
flavor to this tasty
salad.

37

# MARINATED CUCUMBERS

|       |      |                         |
|-------|------|-------------------------|
| 3     |      | large cucumbers         |
| 2     | t.   | salt                    |
| 3/4   | C.   | tarragon vinegar        |
| 2/3   | C.   | sugar                   |
| 1/4   | t.   | pepper                  |
| 1     | t.   | chopped Italian parsley |

Scrub cucumbers with vegetable brush.  Wipe dry.
Do not pare.  Using food processor, slice
cucumbers into very thin slices.  In large,
shallow dish, lightly toss cucumbers with salt.
Combine vinegar, sugar, pepper, and parsley; mix
well.  Toss cucumbers with vinegar mixture.  Cover
tightly with plastic wrap or foil and refrigerate
at least 3 hours or overnight.  Turn into serving
dish.  Sprinkle with more chopped parsley.  Makes
8 servings.

Make your own tarragon
vinegar. See the salad
section for the recipe.

# BONNIE'S FAVORITE
## CAESAR SALAD

| | |
|---|---|
| 2 T. | olive oil |
| 1 | clove garlic, minced |
| 1 C. | whole wheat bread cubes |
| 2 T. | chopped garlic chives |
| 1 | head Romaine lettuce |
| 1 T. | chopped onion chives |
| 2 T. | olive oil |
| | freshly ground pepper |
| 1 T. | herb vinegar |
| 1/8 C. | grated Cheddar cheese |
| 1/8 C. | crumbled blue cheese |

Preheat skillet. Add the oil, garlic, and garlic chives and sauté 1 minute. Add the bread cubes and sauté until browned. Cool. Tear the lettuce leaves and place in a salad bowl. Pour the oil over the lettuce and toss. Add the vinegar and toss again. Add the cheese and bread cubes. Toss lightly and serve.

# MIXED GREEN SALAD WITH STRAWBERRY DRESSING

|          |                                        |
|----------|----------------------------------------|
| 1 C.     | torn Romaine lettuce                   |
| 1 C.     | torn green leaf lettuce                |
| 1 C.     | Bibb lettuce                           |
| 1 C.     | torn Buttercrunch or Boston lettuce    |
| 1/2 C.   | arugala                                |
| 1/2 C.   | walnuts                                |

DRESSING:

|          |                                        |
|----------|----------------------------------------|
| 1/3 C.   | oil                                    |
| 3 T.     | sugar                                  |
| 2 T.     | strawberry vinegar                     |
| 1 T.     | dairy sour cream                       |
| 1 1/2 t. | Dijon mustard                          |
| 1/2 C.   | fresh strawberries (or frozen whole strawberries, thawed) |

In small bowl, whisk together oil, sugar, vinegar, sour cream, and mustard.  Fold in the strawberries.  Refrigerate at least 1 hour to blend flavors.  Arrange all salad ingredients except walnuts on 4 individual salad plates. Drizzle dressing over salad and sprinkle with walnuts.  Garnish with fresh strawberries.  (If berries are really sweet, you may want to cut back on amount of sugar in dressing.)

# PASTA POTPOURRI

| | | |
|---|---|---|
| 1 | | (16 oz.) package dry pasta |
| 1 | | (16 oz.) bottle creamy Italian dressing |
| 4 | C. | broccoli florets |
| 1 | C. | sliced green onions (greens included) |
| 1 | C. | sliced carrots |
| 1 | C. | chopped pepper (green, red, or yellow) |
| 1/4 | C. | chopped dill |
| 1/4 | C. | chopped parsley |
| 1 | | (6 oz.) jar marinated artichoke hearts, drained and chopped |
| 1 | lb. | cherry tomatoes, halved |
| 1 | t. | salt |

Additional (8 oz.) bottle creamy Italian dressing

Cook pasta according to directions until al dente (7-12 minutes); drain. Rinse with cold water and drain. Pour pasta in large mixing bowl; toss with dressing. Blanch broccoli in boiling water to cover for 2 minutes. Drain. Toss broccoli, onions, carrots, peppers, dill, parsley, artichoke hearts, and salt into pasta. Refrigerate covered several hours or overnight. Just before serving, toss in tomatoes and additional dressing.

# SPECTACULAR SUMMERTIME PASTA SALAD

|        |                                                    |
|--------|----------------------------------------------------|
| 3 C.   | prepared vegetable flavored pasta (wheels or swirls) |
| 1/2 C. | sliced Daikon radish                               |
| 3/4 C. | chopped celery                                     |
| 1/2 C. | sliced fresh carrots                               |
| 1/2 C. | sliced patty pan or zucchini squash                |
| 1/2 C. | large chunks green pepper                          |
| 1/2 C. | large chunks red and yellow peppers                |

Mix well.  Add your favorite Italian dressing or vinaigrette.  Chill at least 2 hours.

Garden fresh tomatoes make an excellent salad: slice and sprinkle with chopped basil and grated parmesan cheese.

# LEMON BASIL SALAD

    4 C.    cooked angel hair pasta
  3/4 C.    chopped lemon basil
    2 T.    chopped chives
    1 T.    Italian parsley
    1 C.    sour cream
            Parmesan cheese

Prepare pasta, add herbs and sour cream. Stir
until combined. Refrigerate and add Parmesan
cheese before serving.

Add cooked chicken or shrimp for a tasty main-dish salad.

# SEAFOOD DELIGHT

|       |     |                                              |
|-------|-----|----------------------------------------------|
| 6     | C.  | cooked pasta shells                          |
| 1     |     | (10 oz.) crab meat chunks, fresh or frozen   |
| 1     |     | (2 1/4 oz.) can sliced black olives          |
| 1     | C.  | chopped celery                               |
| 1     |     | (8 oz.) can sliced water chestnuts           |
| 3     | T.  | chopped chives                               |
| 2     | T.  | chopped dill weed                            |
| 2     | T.  | Italian parsley                              |

Dressing:

|       |     |                   |
|-------|-----|-------------------|
| 1/2   | C.  | sour cream        |
| 1/2   | C.  | "lite" mayonnaise |
| 3/4   | C.  | milk              |

Blend dressing ingredients together until smooth.
Mix with salad ingredients.  Add lemon pepper to
taste.

Dill — a natural complement to seafood.

44

# BONNIE'S POTATO SALAD

| | | |
|---|---|---|
| 2 | lbs. | red potatoes |
| 3 | T. | onion, sliced paper thin |
| 3 | | hard-boiled eggs, coarsely chopped |
| 1 | | green pepper, seeded and finely chopped |
| 2 | | stalks celery, chopped |
| 2 | T. | sliced ripe olives |
| 2 | T. | pimento, finely chopped |
| 1 | T. | Italian parsley, finely chopped |
| 2 | T. | chives |

Boil unpeeled potatoes in salted water for 25-30 minutes or until fork inserts easily. Slice into 1/4 inch-slices. Add onion to warm potatoes. Mix together eggs, pepper, celery, pimento, ripe olives, and parsley. Add to potatoes and onions. Add mayonnaise to moisten. Season to taste.

Short of time?

Enhance a deli salad by adding chives and Italian parsley.

## WALDORF SALAD

| | | |
|---|---|---|
| 2 C. | diced apples (unpeeled) |
| 1 C. | chopped celery |
| 1 C. | pecans |
| 1/2 C. | raisins |
| 1 C. | pineapple tidbits, drained |
| 2 T. | chopped mint (also try lime or orange mint) |
| 3/4 C. | salad dressing |
| | sprigs of mint |

Mix all ingredients together.  Garnish with sprigs of mint.

Since ancient times, mint has been associated with hospitality. Plant some by your front door.

# WATERCRESS SALAD

| | |
|---|---|
| 1/2 lb. | watercress |
| 1/2 C. | grated Monterey Jack cheese |
| 1 1/2 C. | blueberries |
| 1/4 C. | toasted pecans |

Dressing:

| | |
|---|---|
| 1 | clove minced garlic |
| 1/2 C. | sunflower oil |
| 1/4 C. | lemon juice |
| 2 T. | sour cream |
| 2 t. | honey |

Toss watercress, cheese, blueberries, and pecans.
Combine dressing ingredients and pour over salad.

Unusual and delicious!
Garnish with fresh
flowers. Read about
edible flowers on
page 6.

# DILLY ZUCCHINI AND
# CUCUMBER SALAD

| | |
|---|---|
| 1/2 C. | finely chopped herbs (Italian parsley, dill weed, and chives) |
| 1 C. | yogurt |
| 1 T. | lemon or lime juice |
| 1 T. | honey |
| 4 C. | fresh cucumbers and zucchini, thinly sliced |

Mix first 4 ingredients together.  Fold in
vegetables and chill several hours.

A refreshingly
"cool" summer salad

# CAULIFLOWER PECAN SALAD

```
1 1/2 C.    cauliflower florets
    1 C.    julienned carrots
  3/4 C.    green pepper
    1 C.    chopped celery
    1 C.    whole pecan halves
    2 T.    chives
            radish rose and carrot curls
```

Blanch florets in hot, salted water for 2 minutes;
drain, and chill.  Keep all ingredients separate
until time to serve.  Then toss together with the
following dressing and garnish with carrot curls
and a radish rose.


HORSERADISH MUSTARD DRESSING

```
  3/4 C.    mayonnaise
    2 T.    drained horseradish
  1/2 C.    yogurt
  1/2 t.    prepared mustard
    2 T.    Italian parsley
            freshly ground coarse pepper
```

Mix well and correct seasoning according to taste.

# LIME SAUCE
## (FOR FRUIT SALAD)

|         |                      |
|---------|----------------------|
| 1/2 C.  | honey                |
| 1/4 C.  | water                |
| 6 T.    | lime juice           |
| 3 T.    | chopped mint         |
| 1 t.    | grated lime rind     |
|         | sprigs of fresh mint |

Combine all ingredients, except rind, in a small
saucepan and simmer for 5 minutes.  Add rind.
Ladle sauce over fruit. Cover with plastic wrap
and chill for several hours.  Garnish with sprigs
of fresh mint before serving.

Make individual
fruit baskets by lining
sauce dishes with
mint or lettuce leaves.

50

# BUTTERMILK SALAD DRESSING

1 C.    mayonnaise
1 C.    buttermilk
1 t.    dill weed
        dash of lemon pepper
        chopped chives and parsley
            (optional)

Place all ingredients into a quart jar and shake
or blend.  Refrigerate and shake again before
serving.

Pepper grass, one
of the lesser known
herbs, adds a hot
radish flavor to salads
and sandwiches.

# ITALIAN VINAIGRETTE

|       |                |
|-------|----------------|
| 2 T.  | chopped basil  |
| 2 T.  | Italian parsley |
| 2 T.  | chopped chives |
| 2 T.  | oregano leaves |
| 1 T.  | lemon juice    |
| 3/4 C. | olive oil     |
| 1/4 C. | wine vinegar  |

Combine all ingredients.  Refrigerate.  Shake well before serving.

A "store-bought" salad dressing can become your own creation by adding chopped chives, basil, or oregano before serving.

# HERB VINEGAR

>     2 C.    herb leaves
>     4 C.    wine vinegar (or white
>                 distilled vinegar)

Wash herbs thoroughly and dry.  Place clean
leaves, slightly crushed, into a glass jar.  (Must
be larger than 1 quart.)  Heat vinegar until steam
rises.  DO NOT BOIL.  Put vinegar in a dark place
to steep for 4-6 weeks.  Filter through
cheesecloth amd pour into sterilized, decorative
bottles.


# STRAWBERRY VINEGAR

>     4 C.    fresh strawberries
>     4 C.    wine vinegar
>             sugar

Crush berries in a deep glass bowl.  Pour vinegar
over the berries.  Cover with a cloth towel.  Let
set for 7 days.  Stir occasionally.  Strain the
mixture to remove residue.  Measure remaining
vinegar and heat over low heat.  Add 1 1/2 C.
sugar to each 2 1/2 C. vinegar.  After sugar is
dissolved, bring to a boil and boil rapidly for 10
minutes.  Pour into sterilized glass "gift" jars
and seal.  (Raspberries or currants can be
substituted instead.)

ENTRÉES

# HERBED CHICKEN WITH RICE

| | | |
|---|---|---|
| 1 1/2 lbs. | chicken breasts, boneless and skinless | |
| 1 C. | sliced mushrooms | |
| 2 T. | butter | |
| 2 T. | chopped chives | |
| 1 T. | chopped lemon thyme | |
| 1 1/2 C. | quick rice | |
| 1 1/2 C. | water | |
| 1 | (10 1/2 oz.) can cream of chicken soup | |
| 2 T. | chopped Italian parsley | |

Brown mushrooms in butter.  Add chicken breasts;
sprinkle with chives and lemon thyme.  Add quick
rice.  Combine soup and water with Italian
parsley.  Mix well and add to skillet.  Simmer
until liquid is absorbed.  Arrange mushrooms
around and over chicken breasts, and garnish with
extra parsley.  Serve in the skillet.

Flowers from the
Chive plant make a
beautiful garnish
as well as being
edible!

# ROAST CHICKEN OR TURKEY

                3 to 4 lbs. roasting chicken,
                           cleaned and prepared
        1/4 C.    soft butter
          2 T.    chopped Italian parsley
          1 T.    chopped sage

Blend the butter with the herbs.  Pat the chicken
dry and smooth the herbed butter over the chicken.
Roast in preheated 350 degree oven for 2 hours,
basting frequently.


A complete roast chicken dinner:  After the
chicken has baked an hour, arrange 10 small red
potatoes, 8 baby carrots, and 1 onion (quartered).
Continue baking the chicken, surrounded by
vegetables, for another 90 minutes.

Sage ⟿
   so compatible
with poultry

# DRESSING FOR
## TURKEY OR CHICKEN

| | |
|---|---|
| 1 | (16 oz.) loaf of whole wheat bread |
| | giblets of fowl (heart, liver, and gizzard) |
| 1/2 | stalk of celery, chopped |
| 1 | small onion, chopped |
| 2 T. | sage, chopped |
| 1 T. | Italian parsley |
| | salt and pepper |

Dry bread in large pan.  Reserve one slice dried bread before covering the rest with boiling water. Cool.  Chop the giblets with celery, onion, sage, and Italian parsley.  Mix in large container with salt and pepper. Mix well.  Squeeze bread slices with clean hands, and combine with meat/vegetable mixture.  Stuff fowl and bake in preheated 350 degree oven for 20 minutes per pound.  Bake remaining dressing in casserole at 425 degrees for 1 hour.

# CHICKEN WITH STRAWBERRY VINEGAR

|        |                                        |
|--------|----------------------------------------|
| 4 lb.  | chicken, quartered                     |
|        | salt and pepper                        |
| 2 T.   | melted butter                          |
| 2 T.   | peanut oil                             |
| 4 T.   | chopped shallots                       |
| 1/2 C. | strawberry vinegar                     |
| 1/3 C. | honey                                  |
| 1 C.   | strawberries, rinsed, hulled, and sliced |

Rinse and dry chicken. Sprinkle with salt and pepper. Heat butter and oil in skillet; brown chicken. Remove to platter with pan juices. Skim fat. Sauté shallots in small amount of peanut oil until translucent. Add vinegar and honey to pan and simmer. Return chicken to pan amd cook partially covered for about 20 minutes. Baste often to glaze chicken. Toss in berries just before serving.

Make your own strawberry vinegar — see recipe in the salad section.

# LEMON THYME CHICKEN

         4       skinless chicken breasts
    1/4 C. to 1/2 C. of "lite" Italian dressing
         2 T.     lemon thyme

Place chicken breasts in a baking dish.  Combine
the dressing and thyme in a small glass bowl and
microwave for 1 minute.  Marinate the chicken
breasts for 30 minutes and grill.

Speak out, whisper not,
Here bloweth thyme and bergomot,
Softly on thee every hour
Secret herbs their spices shower.

                    Walter de la Mare

# CHICKEN AND HERBED DUMPLINGS

| | |
|---|---|
| 1 1/2 C. | chopped, cooked chicken |
| 1/2 C. | chopped onion |
| 1/2 C. | chopped celery |
| 3/4 C. | sliced mushrooms |
| 1 C. | sliced carrots |
| 2 T. | chopped sage |
| 2 T. | Italian parsley |
| 6 C. | chicken broth |

Add chicken broth to a large saucepan (stock pot) and heat to almost boiling. Add chicken, onion, celery, mushrooms, carrots, sage, and Italian parsley. Cover and simmer 25-35 minutes over medium heat. While soup is simmering, prepare dumplings (see on next page). Increase heat to a moderate boil. (Add potato flakes, small amounts at a time, if you want a thicker broth/stew.) Drop dumplings by spoonfuls.

CONTINUED ON NEXT PAGE

A down-home dish........

DUMPLINGS

|       |    |                         |
|-------|----|-------------------------|
| 2     | C. | flour                   |
| 2     | t. | baking powder           |
| 1     | t. | salt                    |
| 1     | T. | chopped Italian parsley |
| 1     | T. | melted shortening       |
| 1     |    | egg, beaten             |
| 3/4   | C. | milk                    |
| 1     | T. | chopped onion chives    |

Mix in order given.  Drop by spoonfuls in moderately boiling broth.  Cover tightly and boil 15 minutes.  Do not raise cover until after 15 minutes, and the dumplings are done.

........ perfect on a brisk night.

# CHICKEN MARENGO

|          |                                         |
|----------|-----------------------------------------|
| 2 T.     | chopped garlic chives                   |
| 1 T.     | marjoram leaves                         |
| 1 T.     | thyme                                   |
| 1/2 t.   | freshly ground pepper                   |
|          | dash of salt                            |
| 6        | chicken breast halves, boneless and skinless |
| 1        | (16 oz.) can whole tomatoes             |
| 1/2 C.   | dry white wine                          |
| 1        | medium onion, cut into wedges           |
| 1 C.     | quick rice                              |
| 1/4 C.   | pimento-stuffed green olives, sliced    |

Combine garlic chives, marjoram, thyme, pepper, and salt. Sprinkle over both sides of chicken. Drain and coarsely chop tomatoes, reserving liquid. If necessary, add enough water to tomato liquid to equal 1 1/2 C. Combine tomato liquid and wine in a 10-inch skillet. Bring to a boil. Stir in onion and rice. Arrange chicken over rice, pressing down into rice. Arrange tomatoes over chicken. Cover tightly and simmer 20 minutes. Remove from heat. Let stand covered until all liquid is absorbed, about 5 minutes. Sprinkle with olives.

# TARRAGON CHICKEN

|         |                                            |
|---------|--------------------------------------------|
| 2       | whole chicken breasts (halved, skinless, and boneless) |
| 2 T.    | butter                                     |
| 2 t.    | flour                                      |
| 1/2 t.  | salt                                       |
| 1 1/2 T.| chopped tarragon                           |
| 1 t.    | Dijon mustard                              |
| 1/2 C.  | dry white wine or dry vermouth             |
| 1/2 C.  | " half & half" (or milk)                   |

Sauté chicken breasts in butter about 3-5 minutes
on each side (depending on size).  Remove to
serving plate and keep warm.  Add the flour, salt,
tarragon, and mustard to pan used to sauté
chicken.  Gradually add wine, stirring to scrape
up browned bits in pan.  Add "half & half" (or
milk).  Pour mixture over chicken.

Tarragon —
adapted from
the French word
meaning "little dragon"

# ORANGE ROSEMARY CHICKEN

| | |
|---|---|
| 6 | half chicken breasts |
| 1 | (6 oz.) frozen orange juice |
| 1/4 C. | honey |
| 1 T. | rosemary |
| | salt and pepper |

Combine orange juice, honey, rosemary, salt, and pepper in saucepan. Cook over medium heat until heated through. Place chicken in glass container. Pour sauce over and marinate overnight. Bake chicken in preheated 350 degree oven for 1 1/2 hours. Baste occasionally with marinade. Cover if the chicken starts to overbrown. Garnish with sprigs of rosemary. Serves 6.

An old English superstition — "Where rosemary flourisheth, the woman ruleth."

# CRISPY OVEN-BAKED CHICKEN

       3 lbs.   chicken breasts, halved
       1 C.     dry bread crumbs
       1 t.     salt
       3 T.     chopped basil
       3 T.     chopped tarragon
     1/4 t.     ground pepper
       1        egg, beaten
       2 T.     lemon juice
                butter

Combine crumbs, salt, basil, tarragon, and pepper
in a plastic bag.  Combine egg and lemon juice.
Rinse chicken and dry.  Dip chicken breasts in egg
mixture and shake individually in plastic bag.
Place pieces in a lightly greased 9x13-inch pan.
Place 1 t. of butter on top of each piece.  Bake
in a preheated 350 degree oven for 1 1/2 hours.
Serves 4-6.

For another flavor
combo ↪ substitute
sage for tarragon.

# PORK ROAST

4 lb.   pork roast
1       clove garlic
1 T.    marjoram
1 T.    sage
        dash of kosher salt
        coarsely ground pepper

Place roast in shallow roasting pan. Rub outer area of roast with garlic. Sprinkle chopped herbs over the surface and lightly salt and pepper. Roast in preheated 325 degree oven for 2 1/2-3 hours (meat thermometer will read 170 degrees).


# GRILLED HAM STEAK

3-4       ham steaks (or pork chops)
1/4 C.    pineapple sage leaves (whole)

Prepare gas or charcoal grill to medium heat. Rub pineapple sage leaves into the steak or chops. Grill until done. The pineapple flavor is more predominant than the sage.

# WILD RICE AND PORK CHOPS

| | | |
|---|---|---|
| 1 C. | wild rice |
| 6 | pork chops |
| 3 T. | cooking oil |
| 1/4 C. | almonds |
| 1/2 C. | Shitake mushrooms |
| 1/2 C. | chopped green peppers |
| 2 T. | Italian parsley |
| 1/4 C. | chopped onion |
| 1 t. | thyme |
| 4 T. | butter |
| 1 | (10 1/2 oz.) can cream of mushroom soup |

Prepare rice. (Cook about 45 minutes in chicken broth.) Brown pork chops. Reduce heat and cook until almost done. Sauté almonds, mushrooms, green pepper, and onion in butter. Add soup to rice and mix in other ingredients. Place chops on top of rice mix. Bake in preheated 350 degree oven for 30 minutes.

Thyme grows wild on the hillsides of the Mediterranean. Imagine the fragrance!

# STATE FAIR HAM LOAF

|          |       |                 |
|----------|-------|-----------------|
| 1        | lb.   | ground beef     |
| 1        | lb.   | ground ham      |
| 2        | C.    | bread crumbs    |
| 1 1/3    | C.    | milk            |
|          |       | salt and pepper |
| 2        |       | eggs            |
| 1        | C.    | chopped onion   |
| 1/2      | t.    | allspice        |
| 2        | T.    | chopped sage    |
| 1/2      | t.    | curry powder    |

Combine all ingredients and put in greased 7x11-inch pan.  Combine the following ingredients in saucepan and heat until boiling:

|          |       |                 |
|----------|-------|-----------------|
| 1 1/3    | C.    | brown sugar     |
| 3        | T.    | mustard         |
| 1/2      | C.    | vinegar         |

Cover ham loaf with half the sauce.  Bake in preheated 325 degree oven for 1 hour.  Cover with remaining sauce and bake 1/2 hour longer.

# TUNA CASSEROLE

|       |       |                                |
|-------|-------|--------------------------------|
| 1     |       | (8 oz.) package chow mein noodles |
| 1     |       | (6 oz.) can tuna               |
| 1     |       | (10 1/2 oz.) can cream of      |
|       |       |     mushroom soup |
| 1/2   | C.    | water                          |
| 1     | C.    | diced celery                   |
| 1/4   | lb.   | cashews                        |
| 1/2   | C.    | minced onions                  |
| 1     | T.    | Italian parsley                |
| 2     | T.    | chopped chives                 |
|       |       | dash of pepper                 |

Reserve 1/2 C. chow mein noodles.  Combine all
other ingredients in a 1 1/2-quart casserole.
Sprinkle noodles on top.  Bake uncovered in a
preheated 325 degree oven for 40 minutes.

Serve with
Dill Cheese Bread or
Drop Chive Biscuits.

See Bread section

68

## ZESTY HALIBUT WITH MARJORAM

```
2 lbs. halibut or cod fillets
          (or game fish)
2 T.    butter
2 T.    chopped marjoram
1/2 t.  salt
1/4 t.  dried red pepper flakes
2 T.    chopped Italian parsley
4       lemon wedges
```

Melt butter, adding marjoram, Italian parsley, salt, and pepper flakes. Pour over fillets. Let stand 5 minutes. Broil 5-7 minutes and turn.

Excellent on the grill!

# STEAMED COD WITH SPINACH

```
   1        bunch spinach (about 3/4 lb.),
                stems removed
1 1/2 lbs.  cod fillets
   1/4 C.   dry white wine
   1/4 C.   whipping cream
     1 T.   lemon juice
     1 T.   chopped tarragon
     2 T.   butter or margarine
            salt and pepper
```

Rinse spinach leaves well and pat dry.  On a 10 to
12-inch plate, arrange about half the spinach in
an even layer.  Place fillets side by side on top,
overlapping edges as little as possible.  Cover
with remaining spinach.  Pour water to a depth of
about 1 1/2 inches in bottom of a steamer or wok.
Place a metal rack over, but not touching water.
(Or use a wide frying pan and empty tuna cans with
both ends removed for the rack.)  Bring water to a
boil.  Place plate on rack, cover steamer, and
cook over boiling water until fish flakes readily
when prodded in thickest portion with a fork (8-10
minutes)  Meanwhile, in an 8 to 10-inch frying pan
over high heat, combine wine, cream, lemon juice,
and tarragon.  Boil rapidly, stirring, until
reduced to about 1/4 C.  Remove from heat or turn
heat to low.  With a wire whip or wooden spoon,
stir in butter and blend constantly to incorporate
as it melts.  (Sauce is thickened by butter.)
Season to taste with salt and pepper.  Pour sauce
into a bowl and keep in warm (hot-to-touch) water
until ready to serve.  Lift plate from steamer and
drain off any liquid.  Drizzle sauce over fish or
serve over individual portions.  Makes 4 servings.

# BAKED COD WITH DILL SAUCE

|        |                      |
|--------|----------------------|
| 2      | cod fillets, frozen  |
| 1 T.   | Italian parsley      |
| 1/4 C. | chopped dill         |
| 2 T.   | butter, melted       |
| 1 C.   | warm skim milk       |

Place fillets into a shallow glass pan.  Mix
together milk, butter, Italian parsley, and half
of the dill.  Pour over fillets.  Sprinkle
remainder of dill on top.  Bake  in preheated 350
degree oven for 60 minutes.

Low-fat and delicious!

# SAVORY PEPPER STEAK

| | | |
|---|---|---|
| 1 1/2 | lbs. | round steak, cut 1/2-inch thick |
| 1/4 | C. | flour |
| 1/2 | t. | salt |
| 1/4 | t. | pepper |
| 1/4 | C. | cooking oil |
| 1 | | (8 oz.) can tomatoes |
| 1 3/4 | C. | water |
| 1/2 | C. | chopped onion |
| 1 | | small clove garlic, minced |
| 1 | T. | beef flavored gravy base |
| 1 1/2 | t. | Worchestershire sauce |
| 2 | | large green peppers, cut in strips |
| 1 | T. | rosemary |
| 2 | T. | chopped basil |
| 1 | T. | oregano |
| | | hot, cooked rice |

Cut steak in strips. Combine flour, salt and pepper; coat meat strips. In a large skillet, cook meat in hot oil until browned on all sides. Drain tomatoes (reserving liquid) and set aside. Add tomato liquid, water, onion, garlic, and gravy base to the meat in skillet. Cover and simmer for about 1 1/4 hours. Uncover, stir in Worchestershire sauce and herbs. Add green pepper strips. Cover and simmer 5 minutes. If necessary, thicken gravy with a mixture of a little flour and cold water. Add drained tomatoes and cook about 5 minutes more. Serve over hot rice. Makes 6 servings.

# BEEF STROGANOFF

|        |                            |
|--------|----------------------------|
| 1 lb.  | sirloin steak              |
| 1 T.   | Worcestershire sauce       |
| 1/2 C. | onions                     |
| 2 T.   | oil                        |
| 1/2 C. | sliced Shitake mushrooms   |
| 1 C.   | sliced fresh mushrooms     |
| 2 C.   | diluted cream of mushroom soup |
| 1/2 C. | sour cream                 |

Brown steak and onions in Worcestershire sauce and oil. Add the Shitake mushrooms (which give the sauce a smoked taste) and the fresh mushrooms. Sauté until golden brown. Add the soup and sour cream; simmer for 15 minutes. Serve over rice or noodles.

Robert Louis Stevenson referred to the onion as "a rose among roots."

# ROLLED RIB ROAST
## WITH ROSEMARY

```
5 lb.   rolled rib roast
2 T.    rosemary leaves
  5     rosemary sprigs(2" long)
        coarsely ground pepper
        kosher salt
```

Sprinkle roast with pepper and lightly with the salt. Place in shallow roasting pan. Sprinkle rosemary leaves over the surface. Place 3 sprigs around the edge and 2 sprigs on top. Bake in preheated 325 degree oven. Use heat thermometer to gauge doneness.

```
140 degrees (rare)-approximately 2 1/2
        hours
160 degrees (medium)-approximately 3 hours
170 degrees (well)-approximately 4 hours
```

# HERBED MEATBALLS

|          |      |                            |
|----------|------|----------------------------|
| 1 1/2    | lbs. | ground beef                |
| 3/4      | C.   | dry bread crumbs           |
| 1        | T.   | chopped thyme leaves       |
| 2        |      | eggs                       |
| 2        | T.   | finely chopped garlic chives |
| 1        | T.   | chopped oregano leaves     |
| 1/2      | t.   | coarsely ground pepper     |
|          |      | oil                        |

Mix ground beef, bread crumbs, and eggs together.
Add herbs and pepper. Roll into small balls (1 to
1 1/2 inch in diameter) and brown in oil; turn
frequently. Simmer until done. These meatballs
are great with spaghetti!


MEATLOAF: Use herb meatball recipe. Instead of
forming into meatballs, shape into a loaf. Bake
in preheated 350 degree oven for 60 minutes. Or
microwave full power for 15-20 minutes.

# STUFFED GREEN PEPPERS

|        |                                      |
|--------|--------------------------------------|
| 3      | large green bell peppers (halved)    |
| 1/2 lb.| ground beef, browned                 |
| 1/4 lb.| sausage, browned                     |
| 1/2 C. | chopped celery                       |
| 1/2 C. | mushrooms                            |
| 1/2 C. | chopped onions                       |
| 1 T.   | chopped Italian parsley              |
| 1 t.   | chopped oregano                      |
| 3 C.   | tomato sauce (or spaghetti sauce)    |
| 2 C.   | cooked rice                          |
| 2 C.   | shredded, mild Cheddar cheese        |

Brown beef, sausage, celery, mushrooms, and onions. Add Italian parsley, oregano, and tomato sauce; simmer 5 to 7 minutes. Combine sauce with rice. Scoop mixture into pepper halves. Place into shallow casserole or pan and sprinkle with shredded cheese. Bake at 350 degrees for 90 minutes.

# MEXICAN SLOPPY JOSÉS

| | | |
|---|---|---|
| 10 | | flour tortillas |
| 1 | lb. | ground beef |
| 1/2 | C. | chopped onions |
| 1/4 | C. | chopped green pepper |
| 2 | | chopped jalapeño peppers (hot) |
| 1 | t. | chopped oregano |
| 1/4 | C. | chopped celery |
| 1 | T. | garlic chives |
| 1 | t. | Worchestershire sauce |
| 1/8 | t. | coarsely ground pepper |
| 2/3 | C. | ketchup |
| 1/2 | C. | French salad dressing (lite) |
| 1/4 | C. | chopped cilantro |
| 2 | | sliced tomatoes |

Brown hamburger with Worchestershire sauce, adding
onions, green pepper, jalapeños, celery, oregano,
chives. Simmer 10 minutes. Stir in ketchup and
French dressing. Scoop onto flour tortilla;
sprinkle with chopped cilantro and a tomato slice.

77

# SPANISH RICE

|        |        |                                    |
|--------|--------|------------------------------------|
| 1      | C.     | uncooked rice                      |
| 2      | T.     | oil                                |
| 1      |        | green pepper, chopped              |
| 1      |        | onion, chopped                     |
| 2      | lbs.   | ground beef                        |
| 2      |        | (8 oz.) cans tomato sauce          |
| 1      |        | (4 oz.) can green chilies, drained |
| 2      | T.     | chopped oregano                    |
| 1/4    | C.     | chopped cilantro                   |
| 1      | C.     | grated Cheddar cheese              |

Cook rice.  Heat oil in large skillet.  Brown
beef, onions, and green peppers.  Combine all
ingredients except cheese.  Pour into greased
9x13-inch pan.  Sprinkle with grated cheese.  Bake
in preheated 375 degree oven for 30 minutes.
Serves 6-8.

Ripe olives can also
be added to this recipe.

# TACO PIE

Cornmeal Crust:

|       |      |               |
|-------|------|---------------|
| 1     | C.   | Bisquick      |
| 3     | T.   | cornmeal      |
| 3     | T.   | melted butter |
| 2     | T.   | hot water     |

Mix all ingredients. Press on bottom and
up sides of greased 9-inch pie plate. Set aside.

Filling:

|         |      |                                          |
|---------|------|------------------------------------------|
| 1       | lb.  | ground beef                              |
| 1/2     | C.   | chopped onion                            |
| 1       |      | (8 oz.) can tomato sauce                 |
| 1       |      | (4 oz.) can chopped green chilies, drained |
| 2       | t.   | instant beef bouillon                    |
| 1 1/2   | t.   | chili powder                             |
| 1/4     | t.   | ground cumin                             |
| 2       | T.   | chopped oregano                          |
| 1       |      | (2 1/4 oz.) can sliced ripe olives       |
| 1       |      | egg, beaten                              |
| 1       | C.   | grated Cheddar cheese                    |

Brown meat with onion, drain. Add tomato sauce,
chilies, bouillon, chili powder and cumin. Cook
and stir until bouillon dissolves. Remove from
heat. Stir in ripe olives, oregano, and egg.
Spoon into prepared crust. Bake 35 minutes in
preheated 350 degree oven. Let stand 5 minutes.
Garnish with grated cheese.

# MEXICAN CASSEROLE

| | | |
|---|---|---|
| 1 lb. | ground beef |
| 1/2 C. | chopped onion |
| 2 | cloves minced garlic |
| 1 T. | oil |
| 1/4 C. | chopped cilantro |
| 1 | (28 oz.) can stewed tomatoes |
| 1 | (1 1/4 oz.) package taco seasoning mix |
| 1 | (4 oz.) can diced green chilies |
| 1 | (2 1/4 oz.) can chopped black olives |

Sauté beef, onion, and garlic in oil. Add the cilantro, tomatoes, taco seasoning mix, peppers, and olives into the meat mixture. Simmer 10 minutes.

| | | |
|---|---|---|
| 1 | package cheese flavored tortilla chips, lightly crushed |
| 1/2 lb. | grated Mozzarella cheese |
| 2 C. | sour cream |
| 1/2 C. | grated Cheddar cheese |

Spread half of tortilla chips in bottom of 9 x 13-casserole. Add meat mixture. Layer Mozzarella cheese and sour cream. Add remaining tortilla chips. Bake uncovered in preheated 350 degree oven for 30 minutes. Spread Cheddar cheese over top. Serves 6-8.

# ENCHILADAS

Meat filling:

            1 lb.   ground beef
            1       clove garlic, minced
            1 T.    vinegar
            1 T.    water
        1 1/2 t.    chili powder
            1       (16 oz.) can kidney beans, undrained

Brown ground beef and garlic.  Drain.  Add
vinegar, water, chili powder, and kidney beans.
Set aside.


Tomato Sauce:

            1       clove garlic, minced
        1/4 C.      chopped onion
            3 T.    oil
            2 T.    flour
            1 t.    salt
        1/2 t.      pepper
            1       (21 oz.) tomato purée
            1       beef bouillon cube
            1 C.    boiling water
            1 T.    vinegar
            2 T.    finely chopped green chilies
        1/4 C.      chopped cilantro

CONTINUED ON NEXT PAGE

ENCHILADAS, continued.....


1           package corn tortillas
2 C.        grated Monterey Jack cheese
1           (2 1/4 oz.) can sliced ripe olives,
              drained

Sauté garlic and onion in oil.  Add flour, salt,
and pepper.  Add tomato purée, bouillon cube
(dissolved in boiling water), and vinegar.  Bring
to boil.  Add chilies and cilantro.  Simmer for 5
minutes, uncovered.  Put 1/3 C. of filling on each
tortilla.  Roll and place in greased 9x13-inch
pan.  Pour sauce over all.  Sprinkle with cheese
and olives.  Bake in preheated 350 degree oven for
30 minutes.  Serves 6-8.

Oregano was known
in the past as wild
marjoram or Mexican
sage.

# SUPER MOM'S SPAGHETTI

|       |        |                                |
|-------|--------|--------------------------------|
| 2     |        | (30-oz.) jars spaghetti sauce  |
| 1/2   | C.     | sliced mushrooms               |
| 1     | T.     | chopped Italian parsley        |
| 2     | T.     | oregano leaves                 |
| 4     | T.     | chopped basil                  |
| 1/2   | C.     | chopped onion                  |
| 1     | t.     | thyme                          |

Heat spaghetti sauce with mushrooms and onions.
Add herbs and simmer 25 minutes.  Serve over
spaghetti noodles.

Fresh herbs add
"fresh" flavor to
prepared sauces.

# SPAGHETTI FROM SCRATCH

|         |                                                    |
|---------|----------------------------------------------------|
| 1 C.    | finely chopped onions                              |
| 2 T.    | olive oil                                          |
| 1 lb.   | ground beef                                        |
| 3 T.    | chopped Italian parsley                            |
| 1/2 C.  | chopped green pepper                               |
| 4-6     | fresh tomatoes (stemmed, peeled, and diced)        |
| 2       | (6-oz.) cans tomato paste                          |
| 1 C.    | sliced mushrooms                                   |
| 2 C.    | water                                              |
| 1/4 t.  | ground pepper                                      |
| 3       | cloves minced garlic                               |
| 4 T.    | chopped basil                                      |
| 2 T.    | oregano                                            |
| 1 T     | thyme                                              |

Sauté onion in oil; add garlic.  Add ground beef
and cook until meat is browned.  Add remaining
ingredients. Simmer uncovered for 60-70 minutes,
until desired consistency, stirring occasionally.
Ladle onto pasta.  Serve with garlic bread.

# SPAGHETTI PIE

|        |       |                                        |
|--------|-------|----------------------------------------|
| 3      | C.    | (6 oz.) cooked spaghetti               |
| 2      | T.    | butter or margarine                    |
| 1/3    | C.    | grated Parmesan cheese                 |
| 2      |       | well-beaten eggs                       |
| 1      | C.    | cottage cheese                         |
| 1      | lb.   | ground beef                            |
| 1/2    | C.    | chopped onion                          |
| 1/4    | C.    | chopped green pepper                   |
| 1      |       | (8-oz.) can tomatoes, cut up           |
| 1      |       | (6-oz.) can tomato paste               |
| 1      | t.    | sugar                                  |
| 2      | T.    | chopped oregano                        |
| 3      | T.    | chopped basil                          |
| 1      | T.    | chopped Italian parsley                |
|        |       | dash of salt                           |
| 1/2    | C.    | (2 oz.) shredded mozzarella cheese     |
| 1      |       | clove garlic, minced                   |

Cook the spaghetti according to package directions; drain. Stir butter or margarine into hot spaghetti. Stir in Parmesan cheese and eggs. Form spaghetti mixture into a "crust" in a buttered 10-inch pie plate. Spread cottage cheese over bottom of spaghetti crust. In a skillet, cook ground beef, onion, and green pepper until meat is brown and vegetables are tender. Drain off excess fat. Stir in undrained tomatoes, tomato paste, sugar, oregano, basil, parsley, salt, and garlic; heat through. Turn meat mixture into spaghetti crust. Bake uncovered in 350 degree oven for 20 minutes. Sprinkle the mozzarella cheese on top. Bake 5 minutes longer or until cheese melts. Makes 6 servings.

# LASAGNA

| | | |
|---|---|---|
| 1/2 lb. | pork sausage |
| 2 lbs. | ground beef |
| 3 T. | oil |
| 1 | (15 oz.) can tomatoes |
| 1 | (8 oz.) can tomato sauce |
| 1 | (6 0z.) can tomato paste |
| 2 C. | water |
| 3 T. | basil |
| 2 T. | oregano |
| 1/2 t. | salt |
| | pepper |
| 2 | beaten eggs |
| 1 | quart cottage cheese |
| 2 T. | chopped Italian parsley |
| | salt and pepper |
| 1 lb. | lasagna noodles |
| 1/2 C. | Parmesan cheese |
| 2 C. | shredded Mozzarella cheese |

Brown sausage and ground beef in oil.  Add
tomatoes, tomato sauce, tomato paste, water, and
seasonings.  Simmer 2 1/2-3 hours.  Cook noodles
and drain.  Beat eggs; add cottage cheese,
parsley, salt and pepper.  Alternate noodles,
cottage cheese mixture, shredded cheese, and sauce
in a 9 x 13-inch pan.  End with sauce and grated
cheese.  Bake in preheated 350 degree oven for 1
hour.

# HOMEMADE PIZZA

|         |                                      |
|---------|--------------------------------------|
| 2       | packages dry yeast                   |
| 1 C.    | warm water (105-115 degrees)         |
| 2 1/2 C.| flour                                |
| 2 t.    | olive oil                            |
| 1 t.    | salt                                 |
| 2 T.    | chopped basil                        |

Dissolve yeast in water in large bowl. Whisk in oil, salt, basil, and half of the flour. Stir in remaining flour. Knead 5-10 minutes on floured board. Place in greased bowl and brush with melted butter. Cover and let rise 30 minutes. Punch down. Divide dough in half. Roll out each half and put on ungreased 12-inch pizza pan Divide the following toppings between each pizza.

|         |                                      |
|---------|--------------------------------------|
| 1       | (14.5 oz.) can Contadina pizza sauce |
| 1 lb.   | ground beef, browned                 |
| 1       | (8 oz.) package pepperoni            |
| 1 C.    | sliced mushrooms                     |
| 1/2 C.  | chopped green peppers                |
| 1       | (2 1/4 oz.) can sliced ripe olives, drained |
| 1/4 C.  | chopped basil                        |
| 3 C.    | shredded Mozzarella cheese           |
| 1 C.    | shredded Parmesan cheese             |

Bake in preheated 425 degree oven for 15-20 minutes.

# HERB GARDEN PASTA

| | |
|---|---|
| 1 lb. | uncooked pasta |
| 1/3 C. | olive oil |
| 2 | medium zucchini, sliced |
| 2 | bell peppers (yellow and red) |
| 1 C. | chopped red onion |
| 2 | medium tomatoes, cut into wedges |
| 1/4 C. | chopped fresh basil |
| 1/4 C. | chopped fresh chives |
| 1/4 C. | chopped fresh parsley |
| | salt and pepper |
| 1/2 C. | freshly shredded Parmesan cheese. |

Cook pasta according to package directions; drain.
While pasta is cooking, heat oil in skillet. Cook
zucchini, onion, and peppers until slightly crisp,
stirring occasionally. Add pasta and remaining
ingredients. Serves 8.

What a treat - pasta
and produce fresh
from the garden!

# VEGETABLE LINGUINE

|        |                                          |
|--------|------------------------------------------|
| 6      | oz. uncooked linguine, broken in half    |
| 2 T.   | butter                                   |
| 2 C.   | shredded zucchini (about 2 small)        |
| 1/2 C. | shredded carrot (1 small)                |
| 1/2 C. | chopped onion                            |
| 2 T.   | chives                                   |
| 1/2 C. | "half & half" (or milk) dash of salt     |
| 1 T.   | chopped garlic chives                    |
| 2 T.   | chopped basil leaves                     |
| 1 T.   | chopped Italian parsley                  |
| 1 C.   | shredded Mozzarella cheese               |

Prepare linguine.  Drain.  In a sauté pan (medium heat), melt butter, add vegetables, and stir frequently.  Cook until still crunchy.  Add linguine, herbs, and "half & half" (or milk). Stir, adding cheese a little at a time until all has been added.

Better is a dinner of herbs where love is than a fatted ox and hatred with it.

Proverbs 15:17

# QUICK PASTA

|         |       |                                                     |
|---------|-------|-----------------------------------------------------|
| 1       | lb.   | uncooked pasta                                      |
| 1       |       | (9 oz.) package sugar snap peas (thawed and drained) |
| 2       |       | (14 1/2 oz.) cans Contadina pasta-ready tomatoes    |
| 2/3     | C.    | toasted pine nuts                                   |
| 1       | T.    | chopped rosemary                                    |
| 3       | T.    | chopped basil                                       |
| 1/2     | C.    | freshly shredded Parmesan cheese                    |
|         |       | sprigs of fresh basil                               |

Cook pasta according to package directions. While cooking, toast pine nuts. (Watch closely; they burn easily.) Combine herbs and pasta-ready tomatoes. Heat on medium heat. When pasta is cooked, drain and combine with tomatoes, pine nuts, and snap peas. Top with grated cheese and garnish with sprigs of fresh basil. Serves 8.

*A tasty and colorful dish*

# CLASSIC PILAF

| | | |
|---|---|---|
| 1 | | small onion, chopped |
| 1 | T. | butter |
| 1 | C. | quick rice |
| 2-1/2 | C. | chicken broth |
| 2 | T. | chopped Italian parsley |
| 2 | T. | onion chives |
| | | dash of garlic powder |

Cook onion in butter in 10-inch skillet until tender but not brown.  Add rice.  Cook over low heat, stirring constantly, for 5 minutes.  Add chicken broth.  Bring to a boil.  Reduce heat, cover tightly, and simmer 20 minutes.  Remove from heat.  Let stand covered until all liquid is absorbed, about five minutes.

Italian parsley has a stronger, more "robust" flavor than regular parsley. The leaf is also flat instead of curled.

# HERB QUICHE

|         |                                    |
|---------|------------------------------------|
| 1       | 9" unbaked pastry shell            |
| 4       | slices bacon, diced and cooked     |
| 1 C.    | grated Swiss cheese                |
| 1 3/4 C.| "half & half"                      |
| 3       | eggs, lightly beaten               |
|         | salt                               |
|         | white pepper                       |
| 1/4 t.  | nutmeg                             |
| 2 T.    | minced parsley                     |
| 2 T.    | minced basil                       |
| 2 T.    | butter                             |

Sprinkle bacon, herbs, and cheese on bottom of
pastry shell. Combine other ingredients and pour
into pastry shell. Dot with butter. Bake in
preheated 350 degree oven for 35 to 40 minutes.
Let set 5 minutes before serving. Serves 6.

A classic quiche

# CREAMY ZUCCHINI QUICHE

| | | |
|---|---|---|
| 1 | | (9 1/2-10 inch) unbaked pastry crust |
| 2 | T. | Dijon mustard |
| 3 | C. | grated zucchini |
| | | salt |
| 8 | | large mushrooms, sliced |
| 1 | T. | minced basil |
| 2 | T. | butter |
| 1 | C. | grated Cheddar cheese, combined with |
| 1 | C. | grated Swiss cheese |
| 1 | | (8 oz.) package cream cheese |
| 1/2 | C. | whipping cream |
| 3 | | egg yolks |
| 1 | | whole egg |
| 1/2 | t. | nutmeg |
| | | salt and pepper |

Preheat oven to 450 degrees. Spread bottom of
pastry with mustard and bake 10 minutes. Cool.
Reduce heat to 350 degrees. Place zucchini in
colander, sprinkle with salt, and drain 5 minutes.
While the zucchini is draining, sauté mushrooms in
butter. Sprinkle 1 C. of cheese into bottom of
pastry shell. Squeeze zucchini to remove all
moisture, and put into pastry shell, fluffing with
fingers. Sprinkle chopped basil over zucchini.
Beat together cream cheese, cream, egg yolks,
whole eggs, and nutmeg. Season with salt and
pepper. Set on baking sheet and carefully pour in
cream/egg mixture. Sprinkle remaining cheese on
top. Bake 45 minutes. Let stand 5 minutes before
cutting.

VEGETABLES

# GREEN BEANS SUPREME

| | |
|---|---|
| 6 | slices bacon |
| 4 T. | chopped onion |
| 1 lb. | cooked green beans, drained |
| 1 T. | chopped fresh dill |
| | dash of lemon juice |

Fry bacon until crisp; remove and crumble.  In 2
T. of bacon drippings, cook onion till tender.
Add to green beans.  Heat and serve.

Dill is a valuable
herb ⌐ it is mentioned
as a tithe in the Bible.

## DILLY BEANS

| | |
|---|---|
| 1 T. | chopped dill |
| 2 T. | vinegar |
| 1 T. | garlic chives |
| 1 lb. | fresh green beans |
| 3 T. | salad oil |
| 1 T. | vinegar |

Simmer first 4 ingredients.  Refrigerate beans in liquid for several hours.  To serve, drain and toss with salad oil and vinegar.

Remember ~
Herbs can be used
as a garnish as
well as a seasoning.

# MARINATED CARROTS

           2 lbs. carrots, cleaned, peeled, and
                      cut into 1/2" pieces
           1       onion, sliced in rings
           1       green pepper, cut in strips

Boil carrots until tender; drain and cool.
Combine with onion and peppers.  Set aside.  Boil
together the following ingredients:

           1       (10 1/2 oz.) can tomato soup
           1 C.    sugar
           2 T.    chopped dill
           1 T.    Italian parsley
         1/2 C.    salad oil
         3/4 C.    vinegar
           1 t.    salt
         1/2 t.    pepper

Pour boiled syrup over carrots.  Let stand
overnight.

*A summertime favorite that can be prepared in advance.*

# GRILLED CHILI PEPPERS

|  |  |
|---|---|
| 8 | Anaheim chili peppers |
| 1/2 C. | finely chopped onions |
| 2 | chopped tomatoes |
| 3-4 | chopped jalapeno peppers (hot) |
| 2 T. | chopped cilantro |
| 3/4 C. | Cheddar cheese |
| 1/4 C. | oil |

Combine cheese, cilantro, jalapeno peppers, onions and tomatoes; mix well. Clean Anaheim peppers, slicing the top off (keep the stem attached). Remove seeds. Stuff with the cheese mixture - press into the pepper shell. Attach pepper "cap" (stem end) with tooth picks. Grill over medium-low heat, brush with oil and turn several times. Peppers are ready to serve when cheese is melted.

Southwesterners say that lemonade will cut the "heat" of chilies.

97

# ROSEMARY POTATOES

|       |                              |
|-------|------------------------------|
| 4 C.  | hot, cooked, mashed potatoes |
| 3 C.  | cottage cheese               |
| 3/4 C.| plain yogurt                 |
| 1     | onion, finely chopped        |
| 2 T.  | chopped chives               |
| 2 T.  | rosemary                     |
| 1 t.  | fresh pepper                 |
|       | dash of salt (optional)      |
| 1 C.  | slivered almonds             |

Mix all ingredients with potatoes.  Pour into a 2-
quart oiled dish.  Brush top with oil.  Bake in a
preheated 350 degree oven for 30 minutes.
Sprinkle with chopped or slivered almonds and
brown lightly under broiler.

Legend says ↪
   After the Virgin Mary
spread her cloak to dry
on a rosemary bush, the
color of the flowers changed
from white to blue.

# HOBO POTATOES

| | |
|---|---|
| 8 | small potatoes |
| 2 T. | butter |
| 2-3 | sprigs of mint |
| 2 T. | chopped chives |
| 1 t. | water |

Place potatoes and butter on a sheet of aluminum foil. Sprinkle chives on top of potatoes. Lay mint sprigs across the top and sprinkle with water. Cover tightly with the foil. Bake in preheated 350 degree oven for 25 minutes. To barbecue, place on grill for 20-30 minutes.

The "fresh from the garden" flavor is restored to frozen peas when a sprig of mint is added to the cooking water.

# ESCALLOPED TOMATOES

|          |                                  |
|----------|----------------------------------|
| 1/4 C.   | chopped onion                    |
| 1 T.     | butter                           |
| 2 C.     | toasted bread cubes              |
| 3        | slices bacon, cooked and crumbled |
| 2        | (14 oz.) cans stewed tomatoes    |
| 1 T.     | chopped basil                    |
| 2 T.     | brown sugar                      |
|          | pepper to taste                  |

Sauté onion in butter, and combine onion with
bread crumbs and bacon.  In a separate bowl,
combine tomatoes, basil, brown sugar, and pepper.
Alternate the tomato and bread mixtures in a
greased, 1-quart casserole, finishing with bread
cubes on top.  Bake 20 minutes in a preheated 350
degree oven.

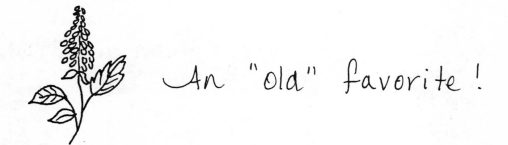

An "old" favorite!

# GREEK SPINACH

```
 2 lbs.  fresh spinach
 3 T.    chopped basil
 1 T.    olive oil
1/2 C.   pine nuts (or walnuts)
 2 T.    Italian parsley
 1       clove garlic, minced
 1       small onion, finely chopped
 2 T.    cider vinegar
         dash of salt
```

Wash and tear the spinach, removing heavy stems.
Heat a large skillet.  Add the oil and nuts and
sauté until golden.  Add remaining ingredients.
Stir, cover, and cook 2 minutes, until the spinach
is barley tender.

A great combination
of flavors!

# LEMON BASIL SPINACH SOUFFLE

|       |      |                        |
|-------|------|------------------------|
| 2     | T.   | butter                 |
| 2     | T.   | flour                  |
| 3/4   | C.   | milk                   |
| 1     | t.   | chopped onion          |
| 1     | T.   | chopped Italian parsley |
| 1/2   | C.   | chopped lemon basil    |
| 1 1/2 | C.   | grated Cheddar cheese  |
| 3     |      | eggs, separated        |
| 1 1/2 | C.   | chopped, cooked spinach |

Make cream sauce with butter, flour, and milk.
When smooth add onion, herbs, and cheese.  Stir in
beaten egg yolks and spinach.  Fold in stiffly-
beaten egg whites.  Pour into greased 1-quart
casserole.  Bake in preheated 350 degree oven
until knife comes out clean (approximately 55
minutes).

 Fresh herbs are
now available year
'round in your
supermarket.

# WINTER SQUASH OR
## PUMPKIN PIE

|        |      |                                |
|--------|------|--------------------------------|
| 1      |      | uncooked 9-inch pie shell      |
| 3      | C.   | cooked winter squash or pumpkin |
| 1      | C.   | milk                           |
| 2      | T.   | chopped chives                 |
| 1/2    | C.   | chopped onion                  |
| 3      |      | cloves minced garlic           |
| 2      |      | eggs, beaten                   |
| 4      | T.   | butter                         |
| 4      | T.   | chopped parsley                |
| 1      | T.   | thyme                          |

Mix all the filling ingredients together until
fairly smooth.  Pour into the pie shell.  Bake in
preheated 375 degree oven for 45 minutes or  until
the pie is firm in the center.

A vegetable
not a dessert!

# FARMERS MARKET SKILLET

| | |
|---|---|
| 3 T. | oil |
| 1 | eggplant or zucchini, diced |
| 1 | green pepper, diced |
| 1 | onion, diced |
| 2-3 | fresh tomatoes, peeled and quartered |
| 1 T. | chopped garlic chives |
| 3 T. | chopped basil |
| 1 t. | thyme |
| | freshly ground pepper |
| | dash of salt |

Cook together until tender.  Stir often so it doesn't stick.

Chopping or crushing herbs before using releases more flavor.

# VEGETABLE FRITTERS

       1/2 C.    whole wheat flour
       1/2 C.    corn meal
                 dash of salt
         1 C.    milk
         1       egg, beaten
       1/2 C.    finely chopped herbs (Italian
                   parsley, thyme, savory, and basil)

Mix first 4 ingredients lightly (lumps don't
matter).  Chill for half an hour or more before
using.  Mix well before frying.  Use any of the
following vegetables:

                 sliced carrots
                 onion rings
                 cauliflower florets
                 broccoli florets
                 string beans
                 sliced eggplant
                 sliced zucchini
        (Watery vegetables do not work well)

Dip vegetable pieces into the batter.  If the
batter does not stick, dip the vegetable in flour
first.  Deep fry in hot oil (350-400 degrees)
until golden and crisp.  Drain on paper towels.
(If the oil smokes, it is too hot).

# TOMATO AND BASIL SAUCE

1 lb.   coarsely chopped tomatoes
3 T.    chopped basil
       pinch of sugar
       dash of salt

Heat tomatoes over low heat to soften
(approximately 5 minutes). Add basil, sugar, and
salt. Purée. Serve with pasta and rice.

Basil ⌐

The ancient Greeks called it the "royal plant" and believed that only the king should be allowed to cut the basil using a golden sickle.

# PESTO

|        |      |                          |
|--------|------|--------------------------|
| 1/4 C. |      | oil                      |
| 2      |      | cloves garlic            |
| 6 T.   |      | pine nuts (or walnuts)   |
| 1/2 C. |      | basil leaves             |
| 1/4 C. |      | parsley leaves           |
| 1/4 C. |      | grated Parmesan cheese   |
| 1/2 C. |      | lemon juice              |
|        |      | grated rind of one lemon |

Use a blender to purée oil, garlic, and nuts. Add
basil and parsley, small amounts at a time. Add
cheese, lemon juice, and rind. Purée until
smooth. Serve over pasta or vegetables.

Pesto— the flavor
of summer captured
in one dish!

# PICO DE GALLO
### (FRESH SALSA)

|       |                              |
|-------|------------------------------|
| 2     | medium onions                |
| 4-6   | (or more) jalapeño peppers   |
| 3     | chopped ripe tomatoes        |
| 1/3 C. | chopped cilantro            |
| 1 t.  | lemon juice                  |

Using a food processor, chop onions and jalapeño
peppers. Add tomatoes, cilantro, and lemon juice.
Mix well and refrigerate.

Serve chilled with
tortilla chips, tacos, burritos,
fajitas ⸜ all your favorite
Mexican foods.

# VEGETABLE LOVER'S DIP

| | | |
|---|---|---|
| 1 C. | mayonnaise |
| 1 C. | sour cream |
| 2 T. | chopped dill |
| 1/2 t. | lemon pepper |
| 2 T. | chopped chives |
| 1 T. | chopped parsley |

Mix all ingredients well.  Serve with fresh
vegetable pieces.  An excellent snack!

In ancient times, dill
carried over your heart
would protect you from
the "Evil Eye."

DESSERTS

# MARIGOLD POUND CAKE

|         |      |                                           |
|---------|------|-------------------------------------------|
| 1       | C.   | butter                                    |
| 1 1/2   | C.   | sugar                                     |
| 3       |      | large eggs                                |
| 1/2     | C.   | milk                                      |
| 1       | t.   | vanilla                                   |
| 1/2     | t.   | lemon extract                             |
| 2       | C.   | flour                                     |
| 1/2     | t.   | baking powder                             |
| 1/4     | t.   | salt                                      |
| 1       | t.   | grated lemon peel                         |
| 4       | T.   | marigold petals, (outer petals of 5 blossoms) |

Cream butter and sugar.  Sift together flour,
baking powder, salt, and set aside.  Mix milk and
vanilla.  Add alternately with flour mix.  Stir in
lemon peel and marigold petals.  Pour in greased
9x5-inch loaf pan or 9-inch tube pan.  Bake in
preheated 350 degrees for 60-65 minutes.  Cool in
pan on wire rack for 10 minutes.  Turn out and
cool.

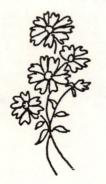

Serve with whipped
cream and fresh
raspberries ↪ a
beautiful summer
dessert.

# PINEAPPLE UPSIDE-DOWN CAKE

|        |      |                                        |
|--------|------|----------------------------------------|
| 6      | T.   | butter                                 |
| 1/2    | C.   | brown sugar                            |
| 1      |      | (15 oz.) sliced pineapple, drained     |
|        |      | maraschino cherries, drained           |
|        |      |                                        |
| 6      | T.   | butter                                 |
| 1/2    | C.   | sugar                                  |
| 1      |      | large egg                              |
| 1      | t.   | vanilla                                |
| 2/3    | C.   | milk                                   |
| 1 1/2  | C.   | flour                                  |
| 2      | t.   | baking powder                          |
| 1/2    | t.   | salt                                   |
| 3      | T.   | minced pineapple sage                  |
| 1      | t.   | grated lemon rind                      |

Cream butter and sugar.  Add egg and vanilla.
Sift flour, baking powder, and salt.  Add
alternately with milk to butter mixture.  Stir in
pineapple sage and lemon rind.  Set aside.  In
ovenproof skillet, melt butter and brown sugar.
Remove from heat.  Arrange pineapple rings with
cherries in skillet.  Pour batter over the
pineapple.  Bake in preheated 350 degree oven for
30 to 35 minutes.  Let cake cool for 5 minutes and
invert on serving plate.

# ROSEMARY ALMOND CAKE

|          |                           |
|----------|---------------------------|
| 1/2 C.   | golden raisins            |
| 1 T.     | rosemary                  |
| 1/4 C.   | cream sherry              |
| 1 C.     | butter                    |
| 1 1/3 C. | sugar                     |
| 3        | large eggs                |
| 1 t.     | vanilla                   |
| 1/3 C.   | milk                      |
| 1 1/2 C. | flour                     |
| 1/2 C.   | corn meal                 |
| 1/2 t.   | baking powder             |
| 1/4 t.   | salt                      |
| 1/2 C.   | slivered almonds, toasted |
| 1/2 t.   | grated orange peel        |

Soak the raisins and rosemary in the cream sherry
for 1 hour at room temperature or, covered, up to
24 hours.  Cream butter and sugar.  Sift flour,
corn meal, baking powder and salt together and set
aside.  Drain raisins, adding liquid to milk and
vanilla.  Add alternately with flour mixture to
creamed butter and sugar.  Stir in raisins,
rosemary, almonds, and orange peel.  Pour in
greased 9x5x3-inch loaf pan (or 9-inch tube pan).
Bake in preheated 350 degree oven for 60-65
minutes.  Cool in pan on wire rack for 10 minutes.
Turn out and cool.

# LEMON BALM CAKE

    1 C.     whipping cream
    3        eggs, separated
    1/2 C.   finely minced lemon balm
    2 C.     cake flour
    1 1/2 C. sugar
    2 t.     baking powder
             juice and grated zest of 1 lemon

Grease and flour 2 (8 1/2-inch) round cake pans.
In chilled bowl, beat cream until stiff.  In
separate bowl, beat eggs until thick and lemon-
colored.  Fold eggs, lemon juice, lemon zest, and
lemon balm into whipped cream.  Set aside.  Sift
together cake flour, sugar, and baking powder.
Fold gently into the cream/egg mixture until
blended.  Pour mixture in pan.  Bake in preheated
oven at 350 degrees for 30-35 minutes.  (Check
with tester to make sure the cake is done.)  To
assemble the cake:  Place one layer upside down on
serving plate and spread with Lemon Buttercream
(recipe follows).  Then spread with 1/2 C. Lemon
Verbena Jelly (recipe follows) or substitute lime
marmalade.  Place other layer on top with top side
up.  Frost the entire cake with the remaining
Lemon Buttercream.

CONTINUED ON NEXT PAGE.....

Thanks to Kathe Abrams,
President of the Twin City Herb
Society, for this recipe.

LEMON BALM CAKE, continued.....


LEMON BUTTERCREAM

       1        (8 oz.) package cream cheese,
                   softened
     1/4 C.    unsalted butter
   2 1/2 C.    powdered sugar
     2 t.      grated lemon peel
     1 T.      fresh lemon juice

Blend cheese and butter.  Gradually add powdered
sugar, lemon peel, and lemon juice.  Continue
beating until of spreading consistency.


LEMON VERBENA JELLY

     2-3 C.    lemon verbena leaves, torn
   2 1/2 C.    boiling water
     1/2 C.    white vinegar
   4 1/2 C.    sugar
     1/2       (6 oz.) bottle liquid pectin

Place leaves in bowl.  Pour boiling water over and
cover with plastic wrap.  Let stand 15 minutes;
strain.  Measure 2 C. into large saucepan.  Stir
vinegar and sugar into infusion. Mix well.  Bring
to boil over high heat, stirring constantly.  Stir
in pectin.  Bring to a full, rolling boil and boil
hard for 1 minute, stirring constantly.  Remove
from heat; skim off foam and pour into jelly
glasses.  Cover with parrafin.  Makes 14 small
baby food-size jars of jelly.

# APPLE BREAD PUDDING

|         |                                   |
|---------|-----------------------------------|
| 4 C.    | bread chunks (homemade or French) |
| 6 T.    | unsalted butter                   |
| 2 C.    | milk                              |
| 3       | eggs                              |
| 3/4 C.  | sugar                             |
| 1 t.    | vanilla                           |
| 2 C.    | peeled, chopped apple             |
| 1/2 t.  | nutmeg                            |
| 2 T.    | chopped cinnamon basil            |
|         | grated nutmeg                     |

Preheat oven to 350 degrees.  Melt butter in 3-quart baking dish (9x13).  Set aside.  Beat milk, eggs, sugar, and vanilla together.  Stir in bread, apple, nutmeg, and cinnamon basil.  Pour all into prepared pan.  Sprinkle with grated nutmeg.  Bake in pan of hot water for 1 hour until a knife inserted in center comes out clean.

Serve with whipped cream flavored with cinnamon or maple syrup.

# NECTARINE COBBLER

| | | |
|---|---|---|
| 6 | | nectarines, sliced |
| 1 | C. | sugar |
| 1/4 | C. | flour |
| 1/2 | t. | nutmeg |
| 2 | T. | minced cinnamon basil |

Slice nectarines into a large bowl.  Add cinnamon basil.  Combine sugar, flour, and nutmeg.  Stir into nectarines.  Pour into a 9x13-inch pan.  Top with the following cobbler.

Cobbler:

| | | |
|---|---|---|
| 1 1/2 | C. | flour |
| 2 | T. | sugar |
| 1 | t. | baking powder |
| 1/2 | t. | salt |
| 1/3 | C. | butter, softened |
| 1 | | egg |
| 3 | T. | milk |
| 2 | T. | sugar |

Combine flour, sugar, baking powder, and salt in bowl.  Cut in butter.  Whisk together egg and milk.  Stir into flour/butter mixture.  Crumble mixture over nectarines, and sprinkle with 2 T. sugar.  Bake in preheated 400 degree oven for 45 minutes or until browned.

116

# PAVLOVA

| | |
|---|---|
| 4 | eggs, room temperature |
| 1/8 t. | salt |
| 1 C. | sugar |
| 1 T. | cornstarch |
| 1 t. | vinegar |
| 1 t. | vanilla |
| 2 C. | heavy cream, whipped |
| | strawberries, raspberries, and kiwi fruit |
| 1/2 C. | edible flowers, (violas or nasturtiums) |
| | Raspberry sauce (below) |

Preheat oven to 400 degrees. Beat egg whites and salt together until frothy. Gradually add all but 1 T. of the sugar, 1 T. at a time, to the egg whites. Mix the last T. of sugar with the cornstarch and add to the egg whites with the vinegar and vanilla. Beat until stiff. Cover a baking sheet with parchment paper. Shape the meringue into a 9-inch circle, mounding slightly, on the paper-covered sheet. Place in preheated oven, then immediately reduce oven temperature to 250 degrees. Bake for 1 1/2 hours, or until lightly browned and dry on the surface. Remove from oven (meringue will crack). Cool completely. Meringue can be wrapped airtight and stored up to 24 hours at room temperature. To serve, swirl the whipped cream over the meringue. Top with fresh fruit and edible flowers. Serve with Raspberry Sauce.

CONTINUED ON NEXT PAGE

PAVLOVA, continued.....

RASPBERRY SAUCE

    1 T.      cornstarch
  1/2 C.      sugar
              dash of salt
  1/2 C.      water
    2 t.      lemon juice
  1/4 t.      almond extract
    1         (10 oz.) pkg. frozen raspberries,
                 thawed

In a saucepan, blend together the cornstarch,
sugar, and salt.  Stir in water, lemon juice, and
almond extract.  Add the berries.  Cook, stirring,
until sauce thickens.  Can be covered and chilled
overnight.

A beautiful, elegant
dessert.  Do not make
on a humid day.

# PINEAPPLE COOKIES

| | |
|---|---|
| 1/2 C. | butter |
| 1/2 C. | sugar |
| 1/2 C. | brown sugar |
| 1 | egg |
| 1 t. | vanilla |
| 1 | (8 oz.) can crushed pineapple, drained |
| 2 C. | flour |
| 1/4 t. | soda |
| 1/4 t. | salt |
| 1 t. | baking powder |
| 2 T. | finely minced pineapple sage |

Cream butter and sugars. Add egg, vanilla, pineapple, and pineapple sage. Stir in sifted dry ingredients. Drop by heaping teaspoonfuls on greased cookie sheets. Bake in preheated 375 degree oven for 10-12 minutes or until lightly browned.

Pineapple sage adds color and flavor to these tropical treats.

# MINT CHOCOLATE CHUNK COOKIES

|          |                                                              |
| -------- | ------------------------------------------------------------ |
| 1/2 C.   | butter, softened                                             |
| 1/2 C.   | white sugar                                                  |
| 1/2 C.   | brown sugar                                                  |
| 1        | large egg                                                    |
| 1 t.     | vanilla                                                      |
| 1 1/2 C. | flour                                                        |
| 1/2 t.   | baking soda                                                  |
| 1/2 t.   | salt                                                         |
| 2        | (4 oz. each) premium chocolate bars, chopped (Ghirardelli or Lindt) |
| 1/4 C.   | minced fresh mint                                            |

Cream butter and sugar.  Beat in egg and vanilla.
Add flour, baking soda, and salt.  Stir in
chocolate chunks (chocolate chips may be
substituted) and mint.  Drop by teaspoonfuls on
greased cookie sheets.  Bake in preheated 350
degree oven for 12-14 minutes.

Two great flavors in one bite !

# SUGAR COOKIES WITH BASIL

|       |       |                     |
|-------|-------|---------------------|
| 1 C.  |       | butter              |
| 1 1/2 C. |    | sugar               |
| 3     |       | egg yolks           |
| 1 t.  |       | vanilla             |
| 2 C.  |       | flour               |
| 1 t.  |       | soda                |
| 1 t.  |       | cream of tartar     |
| 3 T.  |       | minced sweet basil  |

Cream butter and sugar. Add egg yolks and
vanilla. Stir in dry ingredients. Chill dough.
Roll in balls and dip in sugar. Place on baking
sheet. Do not flatten. Bake in preheated 325
oven degree for 10-12 minutes.

*Great for summer ↳
serve with lemonade
or iced tea.*

# INDEX OF RECIPES

## BREADS

## SOUPS

# SALADS & DRESSINGS

# ENTREES

## VEGETABLES

## DESSERTS

ORDER BLANK


HERBS IN A MINNESOTA KITCHEN
10242 Mississippi Blvd. NW
Coon Rapids, MN  55433


Please send me _____ copies of HERBS IN A MINNESOTA
KITCHEN

      @ $12.50 per copy ($10.00 includes sales tax
          plus $2.50 shipping and handling)

Enclosed is my check for $_____, payable to
Benskin, Inc.

SHIP TO:

NAME..............................................

STREET............................................

CITY...................STATE.........ZIP........

       THANKS FOR YOUR ORDER!

----------------------------------------------------

ORDER BLANK


HERBS IN A MINNESOTA KITCHEN
10242 Mississippi Blvd. NW
Coon Rapids, MN  55433


Please send me _____ copies of HERBS IN A MINNESOTA
KITCHEN

      @ $12.50 per copy ($10.00 includes sales tax
          plus $2.50 shipping and handling)

Enclosed is my check for $_____, payable to
Benskin, Inc.

SHIP TO:

NAME..............................................

STREET............................................

CITY...................STATE.........ZIP........

       THANKS FOR YOUR ORDER!

----------------------------------------------------

**A division of Graphco Inc.**

CUSTOM COOKBOOK PRINTING       5616 West Broadway ✦ Minneapolis, MN 55428 ✦ (612) 533-3715